D1348897

EXPLOSIVE

Cliff Todd
EXPLOSIVE

*The story of Britain's leading forensic explosives scientist,
who for nearly three decades investigated some of the
most prominent national and international
criminal bomb attacks in history.*

HEADLINE

First published in 2022 by
HEADLINE PUBLISHING GROUP

1

Cataloguing in Publication Data is available from the British Library

Hardback ISBN 978 1 4722 7896 8

Designed and typeset by EM&EN
Printed and bound in Great Britain by Clays Ltd, Elcograf S.p.A.

MIX
Paper from
responsible sources
FSC® C104740

Headline's policy is to use papers that are natural, renewable and recyclable
products and made from wood grown in well-managed forests and other
controlled sources. The logging and manufacturing processes are expected
to conform to the environmental regulations of the country of origin.

HEADLINE PUBLISHING GROUP
An Hachette UK Company
Carmelite House
50 Victoria Embankment
London EC4Y 0DZ

www.headline.co.uk
www.hachette.co.uk

In loving memory of Vanessa Todd

'No rational cause could be found for the explosion – it was simply designated an act of God. But, thinks Dirk Gently, which God? And why? What God would be hanging around Terminal Two of Heathrow Airport trying to catch the 15.37 to Oslo?'

The Long Dark Tea-Time of the Soul
by Douglas Adams

Contents

Author's Note

To protect the privacy of certain individuals, some names and codenames have been changed. The descriptions of explosive devices are missing crucial details so that this book cannot be used as a bomb-making manual. All expressions of opinion are the author's own honestly held views and are not to be taken as reflecting the views of any organisations the author worked for.

Introduction: The bombers and me

My whole working life has been devoted to investigating the activities of a tiny subset of the human species – a subset who, for whatever reason, have decided to build an explosive device for illegal and often devastating purposes. Some were intent on destroying individuals, others on killing and injuring as many people as possible. Yet more were trying to make a personal statement or a political one. Most intended to shock and draw attention to their deeds as well as to their causes.

They carried out their activities in secret, in fear of arrest, in fear of giving themselves away. Many of them were novices, with only a limited grasp of the technical complexity of the devices they were attempting to build, for whom building a bomb was a matter of guesswork – perhaps trial and error – and thus fraught with as much danger for themselves as for their targets.

Then there were the professionals who'd been doing it for years or had been schooled in a group, such as the quartermasters and bomb-makers of the Provisional IRA,

1

who constructed car bombs, lorry bombs and other such instruments of terror. The arrangement of the key components was broadly similar, but there were always surprises.

In many cases, my work involved devices with unique explosive concoctions and solutions to the technical challenges of supplying power, timing and detonation that had never been seen before. Some bombs were extraordinarily potent, others less so. Some bombs were clever and complex, others crude and simple. All needed careful analysis, understanding and reporting.

In all of my cases, the bombers knew that whatever they did they'd leave clues as to who they were, where they built their devices, what components they used and where they were sourced. They also knew that we would be sifting through every fragment of debris for clues as to their identity and seeking to re-create their unique improvisation in its entirety.

They knew, too, that it was not just me and my colleagues at the Forensic Explosives Laboratory (FEL) who were involved in this work. Alongside us were the security services, the police and army bomb disposal experts.

In thirty years with the FEL, I never came to respect a bomb-maker, but I did sometimes came across handiwork that I could not help admiring.

What I learned above all is that, in this line of work, the devil was most definitely in the detail. One tiny fragment of metal or plastic, a sliver of electrical wiring or a spot of explosive residue a hundred thousand times smaller than a grain of sugar was all we needed to set us on our way.

Let's start with the chemistry.

An explosive is a single pure substance or mixture of substances capable of undergoing a fast chemical reaction, always accompanied by a very rapid evolution of heat, and often of gas. In all cases, an explosive contains all its own energy.

In most cases, the chemical reaction is between a fuel and an oxidiser, the fuel being carbon, or carbon-based, the oxidiser being oxygen.

This can occur within a mixture of substances, such as with gunpowder, which is a mixture of carbon, potassium nitrate (which contains oxygen) and sulphur. Or it can be within a single molecule, such as RDX (cyclo-trimethylene-trinitramine), a pure substance that has both carbon and oxygen within its single molecule.

Mixtures of substances are usually termed low explosives, because their reaction is a burn, which, although fast, is at the low end of the explosive range, and is called a deflagration.

Single pure explosives, where the reaction occurs within a molecule, are usually termed high explosives, because their reaction rate is at the high end of the explosive range, and is not a burn but a detonation.

EXPLOSIVE

Low explosives can be initiated by flame, spark or friction. For example, fireworks.

High explosives need a shock wave to make them detonate.

Prologue

On 7 July 2005, I was one of the first to visit the scene of the London Underground suicide bombing carried out by an al-Qaeda-inspired Islamic extremist on the westbound Circle Line between King's Cross and Russell Square. Accompanied initially by a safety officer and later by Sheila Coles, a colleague from the Forensic Explosive Laboratory (FEL), I made my way along the tunnel in the darkness towards a hellish place where twenty-six people had died and countless others were injured. It was a tumultuous moment in my career that has haunted me ever since.

At this point our escort stopped and told us we'd have to walk through the tunnel. It was a few hundred metres. Having been assured that the power was off and would definitely not be coming back on any time soon, we set off, assiduously avoiding the conductor rail. We must have been given a torch, though I can't remember by whom. We had only been going for a few minutes – I remember that the tunnel had started to curve – when we both heard a rumble that seemed to be coming from somewhere ahead.

What on earth was it? We knew the whole system had been shut down. Was it some kind of echo? We tried to put it out of our minds, though I'm sure both of us were visualising ourselves being crushed as we tried to make our way to the seat of the explosion. Perhaps a rogue train had not been stopped? Had everyone been alerted? We carried on, but the sound got louder and now we could feel the rails vibrating beneath us. This was a very small tunnel, with no more than six inches between the outer skin of a train and the walls.

My memory may be hazy on some subjects, but on this it is still pin sharp. We knew there couldn't be a train coming – there was one stuck in the tunnel ahead of us, for God's sake – but we also knew what our senses were telling us. To hell with this. We went straight for a nook in the sidewall and waited. Sure enough, the noise got louder, and then a light appeared, growing brighter, coming towards us. And something *did* come round the corner – a sort of small, open cart, running along the rails, with several people standing in it.

It turned out that London Transport and the Fire Brigade, between them, had come up with the idea of a mobile rail cart with an electric motor, that could be taken apart, carried on a rescue wagon and assembled on the tracks, for moving people and equipment at times like this. Only no one had told us this before sending us into the belly of the Underground.

So we started waving our torch and, as they came up to us, I could see Roger Morton, another colleague from the FEL, and a Metropolitan Police bomb disposal officer, among others. It turned out they'd finished an initial look at the scene, now that all the living casualties had been removed, and were heading back up to plan the next moves.

Now it was our turn to 'look at the scene'. As we approached the leading carriage, we glimpsed the first hints of the nightmare that awaited us, a nightmare that must have already been faced by victims and rescue workers in the frantic minutes immediately after the explosion. Discarded wrapping for bandages and intravenous fluid bottles littered the track. I could hardly imagine the horrors that lurked in the darkness and dirt and confusion.

The train had just passed through a wider junction and then entered a narrow stretch of tunnel when it came to a halt. There were only inches between the carriage and tunnel walls at this point, but we were able to climb through the opening at the front of the relatively undamaged driver's cab.

The true scale of the carnage only became apparent when we moved through into the passenger compartment. The floor of the central aisle was passable with care, but it was slick with blood and human remains. Bodies and bits of bodies were piled along the seats on either side of it, with little yellow signs saying 'DEAD' on most of the recognisably human ones.

Up to the first set of doors (I think they were still there, despite the wreckage), more bodies were piled on seats with more yellow signs. The floor was getting more diffi-cult to walk on; the handrails had all been ripped off by the blast. And so on, up to the second set of doors – all of which were missing, blown out on to the track where the tunnel widened, where the explosion had taken place. All the windows had been blown out by the blast wave. There was a depression in the standing area where the doors had been. It was hard to tell how deep it was because it was full of compacted human remains. It was hard to walk without slipping over.

The aisle on the far side was much the same, slippery underfoot with more yellow stickers and more bodies. They were piled high on both sides, up to the door connecting us with the next carriage along, which seemed pretty much intact. There was a lot of evidence of paramedic activity, but no more human remains. The tunnel was much wider here, with access now possible from both sides where other tracks merged.

We climbed out on the wider side, into more debris, including the doors and three or four corpses. This must have been where the front carriage had been when the bomb detonated.

Prologue

These bodies displayed very similar damage to those inside the carriage. Although I wasn't remotely capable of making any kind of pathological assessment, observing those who had been close to an explosion could give me important information. High explosives cause specific and recognisable injuries, including traumatic amputation of limbs and scorching of flesh. Clothing tends to be torn and shredded, charred and sooted. It didn't take long to conclude that these unfortunate people had been very close indeed to the blast, which appeared to have been at or around floor level.

We clambered back into the carriage, crossed the aisle and stepped down beside the tunnel wall. So far, the scale of devastation had enabled me to focus on the bodies forensically rather than emotionally, and maintain my concentration on what I needed to be looking for: information useful to the police.

I was also very conscious of needing to stay calm for the rest of the team, to make sure they were managing okay, not being overwhelmed and not needing to go back up to the street. We were all in the same boat, of course, but so far, so good; we all seemed to be coping.

That was until Sheila and I came upon a man wrapped, almost neatly, around one of the train wheels. Unlike the others he was, at first sight, apparently intact, and so was his suit. I suddenly felt short of breath. He was so clearly, so undeniably, a real person, who'd had, if possible, an even more horrific end than those for whom death would have been, if not instantaneous, then at least mercifully quick.

The man in the suit must have been on the far side of the crowded standing area, against the doors, so he would have been shielded quite effectively from the immediate blast. But when the doors burst open, he'd been pushed out with them, most likely still fully conscious and relatively uninjured, and fallen on to the track. The train wheel had achieved what the bomber had failed to do. I remember thinking his head was a slightly strange shape, but otherwise he looked quite untouched.

This image will stay with me for ever, while others, thankfully, remain quite hazy. I'm fairly sure I said something to Sheila along the lines of 'He's clearly not explosively damaged, we'll just note that, and where he is, and move right along.' In other words, 'Let's put him out of our minds and get back into the carriage and back to slightly more tolerable scenes of carnage.'

I'm fairly sure we took one or more of our explosive testing kits on to the track with us. We used them on some parts of the inside of the carriage, more in hope than expectation, since blood and human tissue will fairly comprehensively mask or degrade small explosives traces, but it still needed to be done. Never had I found myself struggling so much just to focus on the job in hand – the forensic investigation of what had happened here. So we looked for the cleanest surfaces we could find, close to the seat of the explosion, and swabbed there for later examination at the lab. We may also have swabbed the detached doors, though I can't absolutely guarantee that. It seems to me, now at least, that that would have been a good thing to do, though with hindsight it wouldn't have mattered anyway, given the nature of the device – but we didn't know that at the time.

Having gathered our samples, and got a fairly clear picture of what we had to deal with, we all headed back to the surface for some lungfuls of fresh air, to take stock, and decide how to proceed.

1

Lockerbie – the best of the FEL

The bombing of Pan Am Flight 103 over the Scottish town of Lockerbie in December 1988, which killed all 259 passengers and crew and eleven people on the ground, was the single worst atrocity that the Forensic Explosives Laboratory (FEL) dealt with during my time there.

What remains the most deadly criminal event in modern British history stunned the world as people confronted the horror of an almost fully-laden Boeing 747 falling out of the sky just half an hour after take-off from Heathrow, bound for New York.

Within seconds of the pilots losing contact with air traffic control, the plane broke up and then came crashing to earth, raining debris and dead bodies all over a small Scottish town where people were watching television early on a winter's evening.

This tragedy occurred just eighteen months after I joined the FEL as a lowly trainee case officer and so it was not an investigation that I took part in. But Lockerbie was always in the background during the following twenty-six years that I worked at Fort Halstead, where the lab was based, overlooking the town of Sevenoaks in Kent, south-east of London.

The Fort was a large and rambling secure complex, similar to a small trading estate, that had originally been built in the late nineteenth century as part of a ring of defensive positions protecting London on its southern flank. By my time it was being run by the Ministry of Defence, which had a number of agencies working there, including the Royal Armaments Research and Development Establishment, which in 2001 became the Defence Science and Technology Laboratory, or Dstl, of which the FEL was a part.

The FEL section of the complex consisted of two main laboratories, one of which dated from the 1950s, while the other was a modern purpose-built two-storey facility completed in the 1980s with distinctive tall extractor chimneys on its roof. Alongside it were a number of ancillary workshop-style buildings, which we used as explosives magazines and storage facilities, where exhibits from the scenes of bombings were kept while being examined. When I started in 1987, there were probably thirty-five employees at the FEL. This grew to around sixty by the time I retired in 2013 – itself an index of how much busier this service became during my years there – of which about twenty were doing forensic casework investigations.

And as I became more senior – I was promoted to head of casework at the FEL in December 1997 – Lockerbie came under my management remit, as we dealt with the various inquiries and legal actions connected with it that have continued to rumble on. Many of these related to allegations of a miscarriage of justice in the trial and conviction of Abdelbaset al-Megrahi, the former Libyan intelligence officer who was jailed for the bombing in 2001.

Some of those allegations were to do with the FEL forensic investigation and are touched upon at the end of this chapter, but they are not my main purpose here. What I want to highlight is what I believe to be – by some distance – the most outstanding example of explosives forensic investigative work ever carried out by the FEL.

The investigation into what happened on Pan Am 103 was led by the then head of casework, Dr Tom Hayes, and his number two, Allen Feraday, who were my first bosses. Tom focused on the analysis of chemical residues, and clothing and luggage, while Allen dealt with electronics and investigations into bomb damage on metals and other surfaces.

Looking back, it seems extraordinary that such a high-profile task was entrusted to just two individuals. Nowadays there would have been at least twice as many case officers involved and probably more. But in the late 1980s at the Ministry of Defence, managers more or less told you what to do and there was very little comeback. In this case their early decision-making, which reflected their concerns about the international political and diplomatic sensitivity of this case, would come back to haunt them.

Lockerbie was quite simply the biggest and most complex investigative challenge imaginable. A huge aircraft packed full of people, baggage and fuel had disintegrated at 31,000ft. While the wreckage was centred over Lockerbie, there were also two long corridors of debris, spread on the westerly wind and stretching 80 miles across northern England and out into the North Sea. In this respect it was quite unlike a bomb attack on a building, for example, or even a conventional plane crash, where the debris field is compact and easily delineated and managed.

What is more, the total weight of the Pan Am plane was in the region of 440,000kg, yet the total weight of the key items of evidence that would show what had happened to it was probably no more than a couple of kilos. This investigation relied on even the most insignificantly small items of debris being found, stored, catalogued and then carefully assessed and analysed.

Tom and Allen took on this mammoth undertaking with unwavering determination and patience, adopting a methodical approach and keeping an open mind about what they were looking at. It involved painstakingly sifting through thousands of items from the aircraft itself and from the luggage it was carrying. They did this work in the months following the crash under enormous pressure, with governments on both sides of the Atlantic and elsewhere keen to establish exactly what had happened.

I well remember those days and Tom, in particular, coming in each day before everyone else had arrived and leaving long after we had all gone home. He spent his time camped out in the exhibit store at the Fort, working his way through an ever-growing mountain of clothing material and other debris. It was hardly glamorous work; he would sort it into piles and then gradually narrow down his focus to the handful of pieces that might – or might not – prove critical to the outcome of the investigation.

It is easy to forget that, in the first few days after the crash, it was not clear that a bomb had been involved. Although it was extremely rare for a jet airliner to fall out of level flight at high altitude while in cruise mode, occasional malfunctions *did* occur. So it was not automatically assumed by everyone that a bomb lay at the heart of this tragedy, and for several days the main theme in the media was the likelihood of structural failure rather than sabotage.

The first challenge, after the recovery of human remains, was to begin mapping and then gathering all the debris into one place. This Herculean task involved mainly the police and the military, but also many civilian volunteers, who picked up everything from tiny fragments of electrical wiring or a circuit board to large components from the plane's interior fittings and structure. It was a joint enterprise that underlined a key aspect of the Lockerbie investigation: that it was, from the word go, a team effort involving many different agencies and even the general public, all of whom played their part.

At this early stage it was the inspectors from the Air Accident Investigation Branch (AAIB) who played the key role. They were allotted a large building at the Central Ammunition Depot – an MoD facility at Longtown, not far from Lockerbie – as a central collection point. Very early on they noticed that one luggage container, with the serial number AVE4041PA, that had been found at Falstone in Northumberland, about 50 miles east of Lockerbie, looked unusually damaged. In other words, it showed evidence of crushing from its impact with the earth but there were also signs that something else might have happened to it first, especially in one corner where the floor of the container was torn and ripped.

This was where Allen took over. After travelling up to Longtown and examining the partially reconstructed container, he selected some pieces of metal from it in order to test them for signs of explosive damage.

You might think that, since the container had hit the ground after falling from 31,000ft, damage from an explosive detonation or from impact with the ground would be indistinguishable. But this is not the case. When a high explosive detonates, tiny particles are produced that move outwards at very high speeds of up to 8 kilometres per second, or 18,000 miles per hour. If they collide with metal or similar hard surfaces within a few feet of the detonation source, they can produce impacts known as pitting or micro-cratering. These are craters often found in metal or similar hard surfaces close to the point of explosion. Some can be quite large – maybe 1–2 mm in diameter – while others are microscopic in size, and they look just like craters on the moon. This is because lunar craters are also caused by impacts from solid objects moving at similar or even much faster speeds – just on a cosmic scale. The point is that nothing, apart from explosively-driven particles, moves at anything near those speeds in a terrestrial environment – including something falling at terminal velocity from 31,000ft. So, if you find micro-craters, you can be pretty sure they must have been formed from a detonating high explosive, and that the craters must have been within only a few feet of the explosive material.

After a series of tests were carried out at the FEL, Allen was able to confirm on 27 December, just six days after the crash, that the metal from the container was explosively damaged. It was a major step forward in the investigation because, although many people involved were already beginning to work on the assumption that a bomb had been involved, they did not know for sure.

Now everyone knew that this was not just an unimaginable tragedy; it was a case of mass murder and the investigation was no longer just an inquiry into an accident and what had caused it, it was also a hunt for the

19

perpetrators. In any exercise of this scale, involving a large number of different government agencies, senior managers are often reluctant to commit resources until they are sure they know what they are dealing with. The discovery of micro-cratering took away any doubts in their minds about where the work on Lockerbie was heading and all the funds needed were made available.

The next objective was to see if there were any traces of high explosives on the metal from the container. Again, it might be thought that when a high explosive detonates, it is all burnt off, but that's not the case either. Some explosives, particularly military grade ones, are very efficient. But none leave no traces of chemical residue at all, so materials close to a detonation will often hold tiny particles of unconsumed explosive.

Now, these particles are usually found in vanishingly small amounts, but there are chemical-analysis techniques that can detect them, and the FEL was, and still is, a world leader in these techniques. And when I say vanishingly small, I am talking nanogram amounts, with perhaps five nanograms being the lower limit of what could be reliably detected. To give you some idea of how small that is, imagine a single grain of granulated sugar and divide that down into 100,000 pieces; each of those pieces would weigh around five nanograms.

After another three weeks of trace analysis, Tom was able to establish that the high explosives RDX and PETN were present in nanogram quantities on two of the pieces from the container. RDX and PETN are commercially-made high explosives, with both commercial and military uses. The levels detected were what would be expected if the pieces of metal had been within a few feet of a detonating charge of maybe a few hundred grams and up to 1–2kg.

One possible candidate was the military plastic explosive Semtex-H, which was produced in Czechoslovakia and was widely used by the military in former Eastern Bloc countries and often contained both RDX and PETN in its formulation. The discovery of the residues on the metal was not proof of Semtex-H, but it was a possibility. Investigators knew it would have been the perfect choice for a small but powerful bomb that would easily fit into a suitcase. The findings only confirmed what the micro-cratering had already established, but now Allen and Tom also knew that a device possibly containing military-grade explosive had been smuggled on to Pan Am 103.

And so the work started in earnest. Hundreds, and eventually thousands, of exhibits requiring detailed examination began pouring into the FEL. These were largely damaged luggage containers, the luggage itself, and its contents. Much of it could quite easily be dismissed as having no obvious explosive damage, but that still left a substantial quantity that required closer examination. And even the stuff that could be easily dismissed still had to be looked at in order to be discarded. Given the amount of luggage carried in a transatlantic passenger plane carrying 259 passengers and crew, even this apparently simple task became a significant undertaking.

As lead investigator, Tom did the initial examination of all of the exhibits, but quickly passed to Allen anything that was even vaguely electrical or electronic, along with any potentially explosively-damaged metal for microscopic examination, all of which was Allen's particular expertise. Under Scottish law, all forensic investigation work must be confirmed by a second scientist. The simplest way of achieving this, in an 'ordinary' case, is for the work to be done together. Nothing about this case was 'ordinary', though, and working together throughout was impractical. Instead, the detailed assessments were carried out by Tom, with Allen then signing them off, unless something unusual leapt out at him. Given the large amount of damaged luggage and its contents, this meant that the bulk of the work, certainly initially, fell on Tom's shoulders.

Although he was my boss, he was only a few years older than me and was then in his early forties. A quintessential English gentleman and highly conscientious, Tom was a wonderful man to work for. With an unflappable temperament, he never raised his well-spoken voice and was always happy to help newcomers like me learn the ropes. He had a lovely dry wit and a mischievous sense of humour that could easily catch you out, especially when you were still getting to know him.

On one occasion, not long after I started work at the FEL, he asked me to join him in the explosives area – a building with massive walls but a flimsy roof, where explosive material could be examined, and where anything that detonated unexpectedly could be confined and not damage the rest of the site. A box of old sticks of gelignite had been delivered for disposal by the police and Tom had gone there to examine them.

Picking one of them up and slowly turning it over in his hands, he motioned to me to come closer to have a look.

'Look at this Cliff,' he said quietly. 'We've got this roll here and you can see how wet it is on the outside.'

'Yes,' I agreed, rather nervously.

'You see the little white crystals – these are quite dangerous,' he added, with an emphasis on the word 'dangerous' that made me involuntarily flinch.

'Oh, they are, are they?'

'Yes, because that liquid you can see is nitroglycerine that has seeped out from the gelignite. The little white crystals are ammonium nitrate, which has also leaked out. If two of the crystals rub together for some reason,' he added, still turning the stick in his hand, 'they can create enough friction to set off the liquid nitroglycerine on the outside.'

By this stage I was starting to back away a bit.

'Oh really? So how dangerous is it, then?' I inquired, trying not to sound too scared.

'Well, it's an explosive – it's dangerous.'

'You mean it could go off if it fell on the floor?'

'Yes, that might do it.'

'What sort of damage would that do . . . if it fell on the floor?'

'Well, the FEL would probably need to recruit another couple of scientists, so we better not drop any of them, eh?'

By that point I had edged even further away.

'It's all right,' he said, with a broad smile, 'you can stand a bit closer, Cliff . . .'

That was Tom to a tee, explaining how we go about things at the FEL, pointing out the dangers and having a bit of fun at my expense.

Allen, by contrast, seemed to thrive on confrontation, was highly intimidating and was combustible when his work or decisions were called into question. He was older than Tom and had been at the FEL for longer than anyone else and he could not have been more different to his boss. But the pair seemed to get on, because, I suspect, they respected each other's strengths, which were perfectly complementary. During my early years at the FEL, I certainly learned to respect Allen's depth of knowledge when it came to electronics and the forensics of explosives.

*

The next step in the investigation was to look in more detail at the metal pieces from the container to see what else the damage to them might reveal. This involved a full metallurgical examination, some of which was done by Allen, but the bulk of which was carried out at a separate department at the Fort that specialised in this and used more-sophisticated equipment than we had at the FEL.

The analysis confirmed that the micro-craters Allen had identified were definitely explosively formed. But by taking sections through individual craters, it showed something else: that there was other material deposited on the floor of some of the craters. In a number of cases this was found to be a layer of melted aluminium, which further analysis demonstrated had originated from one of the side panels of the luggage container.

AVE4041PA, the luggage container, was of a type that has an overhang on one side, designed to fit to the inside curved shape of an aircraft fuselage. From the shape of the piece of metal in question, and the position it originated from in the container, Allen was able to deduce that the deposits in the craters could only have been made if the bomb had been positioned within this overhang. This, in turn, meant that it would have been close to the external surface of the aircraft's fuselage, and hence far more likely to make a significant hole in the outer wall than if it had been close to an inside surface of the container. Of course, the positioning of the device within the container was just a matter of cruel luck for everyone on board.

In any investigation into this sort of disaster, a basic principle is that, as far as possible, every detail should be established and understood so that it can be demonstrated how each component fits together within the whole. In general, the more details that are known and understood, the more confidence there can be in the final conclusions.

In this spirit, the obvious next question was – did the damage to the luggage container match similar damage to the aircraft fuselage and, if so, how could we establish this? The spectacular answer to this question involved the AAIB specialists front and centre.

Over several weeks and even months, the recovered aircraft parts were gradually moved from where they were first stored at Longtown to the AAIB headquarters at Farnborough in Hampshire. Given that investigators knew the luggage container's serial number, they also knew from the aircraft's loading plan that it had been positioned towards the front left of the plane. So, once at Farnborough, AAIB staff set about gradually reconstructing a large part of the front section of the aircraft on a giant scaffolding frame. They were aided in this task by the fact that, on all passenger aircraft, every individual component of the structure is marked with its own unique number, so putting Pan Am's *Clipper Maid of the Seas* back together was like doing a gigantic numbered jigsaw puzzle. While this made it easier, it was still a hugely impressive undertaking that relied on the equally impressive search and recovery operation that collected an estimated four million items of debris from the hundreds of square miles over which it was spread.

As we have seen, this was a quite remarkable logistical and recording exercise, and a superb job was done. But, inevitably, in an undertaking of that size, a few errors in the detailed recording and tracking of the thousands of items did occur. Inevitable though it seems to me that such errors were, some later became part of the ammunition of conspiracy theorists and others who didn't like the outcome of the Lockerbie trial.

The reconstructed fuselage clearly showed that a large hole had been torn in the side of the plane, with the luggage container positioned roughly in the centre of it. More than that, pieces of the structural framework of the aircraft closest to where the container was positioned were examined at the FEL and they too showed specific explosives damage.

The final AAIB report concluded that, initially, a relatively small hole was made in the fuselage by the explosion. That damage then spread, due to the other forces acting on a plane travelling at high speed at 31,000 ft, causing the rest of the structure to rapidly break apart in flight.

Investigators now knew a bomb containing commercially-made high explosive had detonated on Pan Am 103; they knew it was in a luggage container; they knew which container that was; and they knew where that container was positioned and how that had led to the destruction of the aircraft. I should say here that none of the conclusions to this point have ever been in dispute.

Now, the obvious assumption was that the bomb was in a suitcase – could Tom and Allen say anything more about that?

2

Lockerbie: a suitcase, clothing from Malta and a Toshiba radio cassette

Tom and Allen knew that a bomb had brought down Pan Am flight 103. Now they focused on understanding precisely how that device had been carried and detonated. There were two strands to this part of the investigation – the examination of luggage and clothing and what that revealed about the bomb; and electronics.

Taking electronics first: when the AAIB were initially reconstructing the damaged luggage container, they opened up part of one of its crushed aluminium panels and found several small pieces of plastic and electronics rammed into it. They showed these to the FEL scientists at the scene, who realised that they could be very significant, and they were quickly sent back to the lab for closer examination.

It was fairly immediately established that these items had suffered specific explosive damage, and could indeed be part of a device. Because they were explosively damaged, these fragments were all very small, the largest no more than 10–15 mm along its longest axis. Despite this, some still had clear sections of circuit board discernible, and they were big enough for the board material itself to be properly analysed. Allen knew that although the main components of the bomb were no longer present, he had just enough of the board fragments to potentially identify their origin.

It had emerged that Pan Am 103 did not have just travellers from the UK and returning US nationals on board. It was also supplied by a separate feeder flight, Pan Am 103A, from Frankfurt in Germany, and this had brought more passengers and their luggage on to it for onward travel to New York. The transferring passengers would have had their luggage checked through to New York, meaning it would be loaded straight from Pan Am 103A on to Pan Am 103 at Heathrow.

An obvious line of inquiry for the police and Allen was that perhaps the bomb had originated in luggage from Frankfurt. Their inquiries with the German authorities revealed that, during a police operation in Germany in October 1988, codenamed 'Autumn Leaves', a number of improvised explosive devices had been found, designed for use on passenger aircraft, and constructed within Toshiba radio cassette players. These had been made by a Palestinian terror group, and the find was clearly of great interest to the investigation, with much focus by detectives at that stage on the proposition that Palestinians had blown up the plane.

Lockerbie: a suitcase, clothing and a radio cassette

This led, at the end of January 1989, to a visit by Allen to Germany, to compare his bits of circuit board to the intact ones in the devices from the Autumn Leaves operation. In the event, although the Lockerbie fragments were similar to the German Toshiba boards, they were not an exact match. Nevertheless, the similarities were striking. On his return to the UK, Allen made inquiries with Toshiba in Britain, and after much detailed comparison work with them, a match was made with a circuit board from a Toshiba radio cassette, model number RT-8016.

However, Toshiba UK did not have full information on all the company's worldwide products, and they suggested that there were other possible Toshiba models, using similar boards, and that perhaps the company HQ in Japan could help? After a little preparatory international diplomacy, it was arranged for the police and Allen to visit their headquarters in Tokyo, to see if any further information could be obtained. It proved a useful visit, because six other Toshiba radio cassette players were identified that had a circuit board that the fragments could have come from, one of which was the RT-SF 16 'Bombeat' model.

It was now late April 1989 and a month later came a major corroborative discovery – which has since been the subject of some controversy – when the badly damaged pages of a Toshiba RT-SF 16 'Bombeat' owner's manual, with possible signs of explosive damage on them, were identified among the debris from the crash. This strongly suggested that the 'Bombeat' had been the housing for the bomb.

Turning now to the damaged luggage, the focus of this work was to try to identify the suitcase the device was in, what other items might have been in the case and what that might say about who it belonged to, and to ask whether there were there any more bits of the device to be found among those damaged items.

Given the amount of luggage recovered, this was another mammoth task. Firstly, you are looking just for damaged materials and dismissing the rest. This may sound simple, but, as noted above, to separate out the damaged items first, you have to look at everything to be sure that you haven't missed anything. Then, once you have selected just the damaged items, the task becomes much more painstaking and complicated.

Let's start with the suitcases. The object was to find the one in which the device was carried – known as the primary suitcase. Do you just look for the most damaged pieces of suitcases? Yes. But it is more complicated than that. Imagine lots of cases, some of them quite large, all packed up against each other. Wherever the device is positioned within its own suitcase, it is likely to be closer to some parts of a tightly-packed adjacent case than it is to, let's say, one end of its own case. So parts of that adjacent case are likely to be more badly damaged than some parts of the primary suitcase. This is not insurmountable, but it adds a layer of complication.

As well as finding the most damaged pieces of suitcases, you now have to try to identify those pieces that are most damaged on their inside surface, rather than the outside. This is easier with hard-shell than soft-shell cases and, obviously, Tom had no idea to start with which type it would turn out to be. But, ultimately, the primary suitcase was identified as a brown hard-shell case made by Samsonite.

With luggage contents, which were mostly clothing, the goal was to identify items from the primary suitcase, which were also likely to be clothing, so the case would not arouse suspicion if it was opened prior to loading. Damage to this clothing is subject to the same complications as the suitcases, for the same reasons, and it is more tricky to classify than damage to suitcases, because you do not have the contrast between inside or outside surfaces.

So, we have a bomb concealed inside a Toshiba radio cassette player in a suitcase, at least partially surrounded by clothing. As it explodes, fragments are rammed into whatever they are next to. Then those combined fragments are further rammed into what they are next to, and so on. Although you do get individual pieces of debris, those which are closest to a bomb tend to be compressed fragments of different materials. And if you select those pieces that contain bits of the device – any type of rigid, mechanical or electrical materials – but do not include any suitcase shell, you can be reasonably sure that they originated from the primary suitcase. By doing this you are essentially removing the outer layer of materials in the primary suitcase from your most robust findings, but that is the safest way to proceed, and that is what was done by Tom and Allen. Everything else was still examined in detail and reported, but with the caveat that it *may* not have originated from the primary suitcase.

It was a meticulous and time-consuming business and it wore Tom down, as he was also having to deal with his other responsibilities as head of casework. It has always seemed to me that more should have been done to ensure the load was sustainable.

And after all this time and effort – what results? Several items of clothing were identified as coming from the primary suitcase, most of which had fragments of a Toshiba radio cassette embedded within them, some of which included fragments of the owner's manual.

Three items of clothing, however, were of particular importance to the investigation. One was a blue-and-white babygro that had a label on it indicating it was made in Malta. Another was a pair of trousers bearing a 'Yorkie' brand label, and also another label with a printed number still visible. The babygro led to extensive police inquiries in Malta, to see if its source could be tracked down further.

Initially it seemed that this would not take the investigation much further, as that particular babygro was distributed quite widely, not just in Malta. But a little while later, with help from the US authorities, the 'Yorkie' brand trousers were also tracked down to a factory in Malta. When the police returned to Malta to visit that factory, they were told that the label with the printed number was a factory batch number – and that whole batch had been sold to a shop called Mary's House in Sliema, a town in Malta, in November 1988, the month before the bombing.

This was the start of a big leap forward in the police investigation, but there was a third very significant find among the clothing. This was the discovery of a fragment of cloth from a 'Slalom'-brand shirt. It was heavily creased and folded, but when dissected open it was found to contain a few small pieces of plastic, paper and a fragment of a circuit board. This fragment was clearly explosively damaged, but, crucially, it was of a completely different type to the Toshiba boards.

Tom found it in May 1989, five months after the crash, and gave it to Allen, who would have known very quickly that this was not from a Toshiba board. He knew that, to work as a bomb, the Toshiba would have had to be modified in some way and that this fragment could very likely be part of that modification and so was a very significant item.

It is not mentioned again in any FEL files until September of 1989, when Allen sent a memo to the police asking for their help in tracking down its source. I don't know this as fact, but probably during this time he would have been examining every database he had access to, trying every contact he had, and every test he could think of, to try to trace its origin himself, because this would very likely throw the case wide open, which would be a major feather in his cap.

In the event, he was unable to trace it, hence the memo. With hindsight, it probably would have been better to immediately ask for that help at the same time as pursuing his own inquiries, but I understand the human instinct of trying to be first, and the point of hindsight is that we none of us have the benefit of it at the time.

Following that memo, the fragment was the subject of a worldwide search and testing by many parties, but it wasn't until a conference in June 1990, where details were given to the FBI, who had access to even more databases – including a CIA one – that any database threw up a match.

The upshot of all of this is that it was not until September 1990 that the board was provisionally identified as being of the MEBO brand, a small company in Switzerland. More international diplomacy and legal hurdles followed, but, in November 1990, the police visited the MEBO factory and took away several samples for comparison with the fragment. As a result, it was positively identified as part of a MEBO timer board, programmable for up to ninety-nine hours before it would perform some action, such as providing power to a firing circuit.

This fragment and the evidential trail linking it to Libya

would play a major role in the prosecution of al-Megrahi and a second man, Lamin Fhimah, who was acquitted at the 2001 trial. It has since become the focus of intense speculation and conspiracy theorising about the way it was found by Tom, about its origin and its compatibility with MEBO timers, but I had – and still have – no doubt whatsoever that the original conclusions made about it were, and still are, accurate.

This huge investigative task inevitably took its toll on Tom, but his sudden resignation from the FEL in early 1990 still took us all by surprise and it came as a big shock to me. Despite his repeated warnings to senior management that his workload was unsustainable, nothing had changed. When he handed in his notice there was a palpable sense within the lab of mild panic amongst that management, but the damage was done, and Tom walked away from the FEL and went off to retrain as a chiropodist. To me this was an entirely avoidable and tragic waste of a very skilled and committed forensic scientist.

He and Allen – who succeeded him as head of casework – had conducted an extraordinary investigative process that played an important role in the conviction of al-Megrahi, who was sentenced to life in prison, but has since died after being released on compassionate grounds.

When I became head of casework at the FEL, I made it my business to go back through all the paperwork covering what they had done. There were a number of reasons why

I did this, one of which was in order to answer the various questions that continued to be posed to the FEL long after Tom and Allen had left the service. I also wanted to present the story of what they had done to the rest of the FEL staff, almost all of whom were too young by that time to have had any knowledge of them or their investigation. It was not only a great example of the FEL at its best, but also a way of ensuring that the lessons learned from Lockerbie were handed on to new generations of forensic explosives scientists.

There was a further reason, and a much more personal one. Far from being lauded for their skill and dedication, much of what has since been written about Tom and Allen's work on Lockerbie has been highly critical, implying at the least incompetence, and at the worst outright dishonesty. For example, Tom has been accused of fabricating or changing some of his notes to fit the prosecution's case, and Allen of either getting his conclusions about the timer fragment wrong or, worse, incorporating the timer fragment dishonestly into the evidence chain, again to suit the prosecution's case.

In my opinion all these criticisms are baseless. I say that from first-hand knowledge of the characters themselves, and close second-hand knowledge of their forensic work, which I believe makes me far better informed than most critical commentators. To me it still rankles that, so far as I am aware, nothing has been publicly written to directly dispute these allegations, which have obscured so much good work. I simply could not leave this aspect of the Lockerbie investigation untouched.

So I will finish with just one observation. Starting in September 2003 and finishing almost four years later in June 2007, the Scottish Criminal Cases Review Commission (SCCRC) conducted a detailed review of every aspect of the Lockerbie investigation and trial. Materials they accessed included the trial transcript, all Crown and defence trial documents, all 15,000 police witness statements, all defence solicitors' correspondence and witness files, and all the FEL files and materials. They conducted inquiries in the UK, Malta, Libya and Italy, and interviewed forty-five witnesses and experts, including Tom and Allen, as well as the two accused.

In all, the SCCRC were presented with forty-eight separate grounds where a possible miscarriage of justice may have occurred, and hence should be referred for appeal. In relation to forty-five of those grounds, they did not believe a miscarriage of justice had occurred. In relation to three grounds, plus another three it identified for itself, it considered that a miscarriage of justice may have occurred, giving a total of six grounds.

Of those six grounds for a possible appeal – which never took place because of the release of al-Megrahi on compassionate grounds – five of them had nothing to do with Tom and Allen's work. That leaves one, which concerns a document that was not disclosed at the original trial but the contents of which have remained secret for legal reasons. Whether that document refers to Allen or Tom or their work remains a matter of speculation, but it seems highly unlikely, given the confidence expressed by the SCCRC report in them in all other respects.

3

My first car bomb

I was in the examination laboratory at the Fort. A large, rectangular space with benches along the walls, it had a number of island worktops placed widthwise across the room. I was at one of them, having just retrieved several evidence bags from the store containing parts of a device in my latest case, ready to examine each in detail. As I made a start, the lab door opened and Allen Feraday walked in.

By June 1990, he had been head of casework for just under six months and I was immediately on my guard. I was still quite junior at the FEL and was only just starting to take on some of my own cases.

Up until then I had had little interaction with Allen, because initially he had not been in my management chain. What contact I had had with him, in my mind at least, had not gone well. But with the recent upheavals and Tom Hayes' departure, that had all changed; Allen was now overseeing my work too and he made me feel nervous.

He spotted me and came over. Thank God he was in a good mood.

'Ah, there you are, Cliff. Not too busy, I hope?'

I mumbled something positive-sounding as he went on, barely waiting for my response.

'I've got a nice little job for you. Pack all that stuff away, lad. You're off down to Wiltshire.'

'Wiltshire?'

'Yes. A car has exploded and caught fire, and the fire brigade think it's suspicious, so the police want a forensic scientist to take a look – and the Met have lent them a helicopter to get you there. It'll be waiting for you at Biggin Hill, so get someone to drive you over there and you are on your way. Oh, and take Simon Morrison with you. It'll be good experience for him to see what we do here.'

Simon was the latest recruit to the FEL, and had only been with us for a month or so, but he was the least of my concerns. My new boss's instructions had left me feeling dumbfounded. I hardly knew where to start.

'Err, well, okay . . . but I've never been to a car-bomb scene before,' I offered weakly.

'Well, there you are, then: the perfect opportunity to get some experience,' came Allen's thumping reply. 'You'll be fine, lad. You know what kind of bits – and what sort of damage – to look for. You better get started. Don't want to keep the helicopter waiting.'

And then he was gone, leaving me in a state of nervous apprehension and adrenalin-pumping excitement. Not only was this my first possible car bomb, it was also my first solo explosives scene of any kind representing the FEL, and I would be the one making the decisions.

It would be an experience that taught me that what you learn in training or from textbooks is not often matched by what you find in the real world. This case would also be my first experience of dealing with a victim of explosives – something that was entirely overlooked in my training, where the focus was exclusively on the forensic chemistry of 'devices', not on the people they were intended to maim or kill. I would discover that victims do not always make for reliable witnesses.

I stumbled around the lab, packing a bag with a few small tools, a trace explosives swabbing kit, exhibit bags, some disposable overalls and gloves, and general stationery, and then went and found Simon. I was thinking: 'This is great – the partially sighted leading the totally blind. What could possibly go wrong?'

Biggin Hill is only a few miles from the Fort, and one of our support staff was happy to give us a lift. Within 40 minutes of Allen's intervention, we were climbing aboard the helicopter. It was smaller than I was expecting, the size of a small saloon car, with two seats in the front and two in the back, which is where we sat. I'd never been in a chopper before, so I was looking forward to the ride.

In front it was just the pilot. I assumed the passenger seat was usually occupied by a navigator, but, on that day, somewhat to our amusement, it turned out that navigation was supplied courtesy of *Bartholomew's Road Atlas of Great Britain*. The pilot simply followed the main roads and just cut large corners off whenever he needed to make a turn.

In that rather haphazard manner, we made our way on a wet day down to west Wiltshire, arriving after about an hour over a field outside the village of Winterslow near Salisbury. A police car was waiting and there were people waving us over in one corner by a gate. After setting down and waiting for us to get clear, the pilot took off immediately and headed for home. We were going to have to make our own way back. The fun part of the day was over and the nervous apprehension was kicking in.

I can't be sure now, but I think we were able to walk from where we landed to the place where the burnt-out shell of a Suzuki Santana jeep was sitting on its axles on an unmade track. This led to the driveway of an elegant period house standing on its own at the end of a lane, where, I gathered, the female driver of the jeep lived.

By the time we got to the scene the fire brigade had been and gone, after putting out a blaze that had reached a fierce temperature, burning almost all the paint off the jeep's bodywork. The acrid smell of a burnt-out car filled the damp air. The two rear tyres of the Suzuki were burned away, all the windows had gone and all the doors and body panels had bulged out. The shell was soaked not only with water from the fire engine but from the steadily falling rain and I could see that much of the debris from the fire, and whatever had caused it, had sunk into the mud.

My heart sank. 'Oh well,' I thought, 'at least I can be sure of one thing – there has definitely been an explosion of some kind.'

Having seen the general condition of the jeep, the police had called army bomb disposal and I was relieved to find an officer in army fatigues still there. I was hoping he would help answer the key questions – was this a bomb of some kind and, if so, what? Or was it, as the police and vehicle's owner initially suspected, a petrol explosion caused by some kind of malfunction in the car itself?

After introducing myself and eagerly asking him what he thought had happened, I got short shrift.

'I dunno, mate,' he said. 'I suppose it could have been a petrol explosion. Not sure how you could tell looking at the state of it now. But if it was some kind of bomb, I'm quite sure there is no live material left. It's all safe now as far as that goes, so I'm off now. Good luck with it.'

It was not the reply I had been hoping for. Then, just to add to my discomfort, the policeman who had briefed me on the way over to the scene asked me if I would like to speak to the victim.

Under the circumstances, it was a fair question and based on a reasonable expectation that that was something I would want – or need – to do. But at this point in my career I had never interviewed anyone about anything, let alone someone who had just survived a terrifying experience that may have been deliberately designed to injure or kill them.

'Well, yes,' I replied uncertainly, 'if she feels up to it, I probably would like to speak to her, but I had better take a proper look at the car first.'

I was playing for time, but this was also the right way to proceed. Although I felt out of my depth, I realised that even with my limited experience I knew more about what I should be looking for than anyone else on hand that day. And with that thought in mind, I put on my disposable overalls and gloves, instructed Morrison to do the same, and we approached the jeep.

Initially I moved forward alone and very carefully, making sure that I watched where I was putting my feet, and noting what route I was taking so I could take the same route back, and not deviate. This is standard practice, certainly at explosion scenes and most crime scenes, when you aim to disturb things as little as possible. However, it pretty soon dawned on me that the ground all around the jeep was well and truly trampled, not least by the fire brigade. So while still being careful, I beckoned Simon to join me and we relaxed enough to have a thorough look at the car and all around it.

As we had seen from a distance, the bulging state of the body panels indicated an internal explosion of some sort, and up close we could see that the fire had completely destroyed the inside of the jeep. The bonnet was particularly misshapen, especially around the area of the catch where it shuts. But I had already been told that much of that damage had been caused by the fire brigade when forcing it open to douse the fire in the engine compartment.

Most interesting to me was a large hole that had been torn in the floor behind the driver's seat, with the floor pan pushed up inside the car. That again confirmed that a significant explosion had taken place. It might also have suggested that the explosion happened underneath the floor pan, but I already knew enough to not immediately make that assumption. When an explosion happens to a car, the blast is reflected by its proximity to the ground back up into the car, whether or not it started inside or outside the car, so the floor pan almost always ends up pushed up into the car. But, I wondered, could a petrol explosion, caused by a ruptured fuel line, for example, really cause that sort of damage? And how could that have occurred? What I really needed to find were some bits of debris that clearly did not come from the jeep itself.

While I was walking around the wreckage I had noticed one piece of twisted metal that seemed to be painted red on one side, and was not an obvious part of the car. 'Wow, that looks odd,' I thought. 'I wonder whether that is the key to this.' But during this initial assessment I left it where it was.

The main problem, I now realised, was that it was almost impossible to see or access the underside of the vehicle because it was sitting in the mud. We needed to get it lifted and see what was underneath.

Simon and I headed towards the house where the policeman escorting us was waiting. I could tell he was expecting a decision from me. My first time alone at a scene and I had to make a judgement that I knew would have a major bearing on how this investigation panned out. There was no doubt in my mind an explosion had occurred but I could not be sure why. What if it was just a one-off technical malfunction in the car? In that case I'd look pretty silly having it lifted and escorted under wraps to the Fort in preparation for a full forensic examination.

Part of the problem was that the damage I could see was not consistent with the photographs of car bombs I had studied at the FEL. Nor was it similar to the damage inflicted on the car of Tory MP Airey Neave, who had been killed by an IRA bomb in Westminster eleven years earlier. That car was still stored at the Fort and I'd had a close look at it. It and the cars in the photos showed evidence of high explosive creating a clean cutting, or shearing action on the bodywork, whereas this jeep seemed to have suffered more of a tearing pattern that was hard to reconcile with a high-explosive bomb.

'I just can't see any plausible mechanism by which an accidental petrol leak could have caused this,' I said to Simon as we walked towards the house.

'Yeah, cars just don't do this, do they,' he offered.

My first car bomb

It was instinct as much as anything. The evidence pointed towards an explosion and it seemed a remote possibility that it had not been caused by a bomb of some kind. I decided to err on the side of caution.

'Yep. Right,' I told Simon. 'We can't rule out a bomb, so we need to get this back to the lab.'

I reached the policeman and, sounding as confident as I could, informed him this was most likely damage caused by a device of some sort and that we now needed to lift the car on to a tow-truck, with it sheeted, top to bottom, in tarpaulins, ready for the journey to Sevenoaks. They would also need some scene-of-crime officers to search and recover all the debris remaining, after the car had been removed. I just hoped that I was right, because this was going to cost them significant money and resources.

In the meantime, I had to face up to what I was really not looking forward to – speaking to the victim. I had learned from the police officer that this was a female veterinary scientist in her forties who worked at the nearby government weapons research establishment at Porton Down. She had made an almost miraculous escape by climbing out of the driver's window when the jeep caught fire, having at first tried and failed to open the door. How close she came to serious injury was underlined by the singeing of her hair on the back of her head and the state of her anorak, which was melted across the shoulders and the hood. I later calculated she would have had about ten seconds to escape before she would have been overwhelmed by fumes and heat.

My stage fright at this first encounter with a victim proved entirely unnecessary. When I was ushered in to see Margaret Baskerville, I found her in an impressively self-possessed mood.

'I'm sorry to intrude on what must have been a very difficult morning for you,' I offered tamely, as I took a seat opposite her in the sitting room. I was thinking that 'difficult' might not have been the right word. More like 'frightening' or 'terrifying'. But she appeared not the least bit concerned. If anything she sounded almost apologetic for taking up my time.

'Really, that is no problem at all. How can I help you?'

'Well, perhaps you could explain what you recall happened when you got in the jeep?'

'Well, I got into the jeep as normal and reversed out of the drive on to the track and braked, ready to move forward. Then I remember hearing this sudden whooshing sound, and the next thing I knew the whole thing was on fire.'

'A whooshing sound? No bang?'

My mind was racing. What she was describing was consistent with a petrol fire, not a bomb explosion. When petrol ignites it sucks the oxygen out of the air. If you are close to the ignition point, you feel a sensation just as she described – a whooshing sound or whump! as the vapour ignites and bursts into flames.

'Are you sure there was no bang?'

'No, Mr . . . ?'

'Todd.'

'No, Mr Todd, I don't recall a bang. Maybe a sort of thump but not a bang . . .'

She then described how she felt the growing heat developing behind her and how she managed to get out, all the time assuming something had gone wrong with the car.

How could that be, I wondered, as Simon and I went back outside. Had I missed something and jumped the gun here? Still, the die was cast, and soon a recovery lorry arrived with a large hydraulic crane on the back. Because we couldn't get underneath the car, straps were passed through its door windows and it was lifted up by its roof. A large tarpaulin was then placed underneath, to catch anything that might drop off, and lashed together over its roof, and in this state it was placed on the back of the lorry.

Now we had clear access to the ground underneath – and very soon I could breathe a sigh of relief. Among several bits of metal that did not look as though they came from the car were several pieces of shattered magnetic material that I was quite familiar with from under-car devices I had seen at the FEL.

This was ferrite, a dark, hard, brittle ceramic material of iron mixed with one or more other metallic elements to make powerful permanent magnets. These come in a variety of commercial forms, including 'Sea Searcher' magnets used by divers to retrieve tools from the ocean floor. There could be little doubt – something had been attached to the underside of this vehicle.

This was now definitely a crime scene and there was, naturally, some discussion about who might have done this and why Mrs Baskerville had been targeted. The police were aware that she worked at Porton Down and it was only then that I heard suggestions that her job involved helping to look after animals involved in experiments. This immediately pointed to animal welfare extremists, though car-bombing was not their normal modus operandi. But, to be frank, my focus that day was purely on what had happened on that track, not who had done it.

We had arrived in Wiltshire by helicopter, but Simon and I now had to make our own, rather more mundane, way back to the Fort by train after getting a lift with the police to the nearest station.

The following day, the car and much of the debris that was collected from the police search was delivered to the FEL and the process of carefully examining everything from the scene began. The goal at that stage was to give the police some useful information to guide their investigation, and also to settle some of the many questions in my own mind about what had happened. In this I was encouraged by the reaction of some of the more senior case officers whom I invited to look at the car. They generally agreed that this was not the sort of damage you would expect from a high-explosive device, attached with powerful magnets.

Then, four days later, on the following Sunday, something happened in Bristol that not only transformed the scale of this inquiry but also helped me answer many of the central questions I was wrestling with from Wiltshire.

That morning Dr Max Headley, an animal researcher at the University of Bristol, was driving along Cotham Road, a residential street in the middle of the city, when a bomb detonated under or just behind his red VW Golf. The car came to rest about fifty yards further on from the detonation point. While Dr Headley escaped unhurt, a thirteen-month-old baby boy being wheeled along the pavement in his pushchair by his father was not so lucky. In fact, he was incredibly unlucky: John Cupper suffered flash burns, a partially severed finger and shrapnel wounds to his back.

I was at work at the time – in on a Sunday trying to get to grips with the Wiltshire bomb when I took the call. The policeman in charge asked if I could get down to Bristol, but, with no helicopter available, I decided the best use of my time was to stay where I was. Instead I would talk them through what I needed them to do at the scene.

In this case – crucially – there was no fire. There was no doubt that a bomb had detonated because the car showed all the signs of that – bulging bodywork, blown-out windows – and the debris was easy to find on a tarmac road bordered by pavements. So we needed a thorough search and collection process and the car to be wrapped and transported to the Fort.

The press and everyone else involved in the investigation immediately connected the two events and blamed animal rights extremists. The *Daily Mirror* even offered a £5,000 reward for information leading to the perpetrators of both attacks and the Research Defence Society offered £10,000. The police received a call from someone claiming to represent the Animal Liberation Front claiming responsibility – a call that they took seriously.

Within 48 hours it emerged that Dr Headley had been driving around Bristol for two days with the bomb under his car without it detonating. A neighbour had spotted a box-like device under the VW but had assumed it was some sort of legitimate attachment to the car. Even so, he had informed the police, who had not then followed up with Dr Headley.

On the Sunday, Dr Headley had driven for about a mile when he started hearing a rumbling sound. The police believed that at this point the box containing the bomb had partially detached, triggering the explosion two or three feet behind the handbrake mounting. On this occasion the bomb had been placed under the passenger seat, which was ripped off its mountings with a hole in the floor underneath. Once again the intended victim had been very lucky not to have been seriously injured or killed.

Two days later, the VW and all its associated debris arrived at the FEL. This was a big step forward in enabling me to establish what the device was in each case, how they had worked, and whether they were largely identical. Because there was no fire in Bristol, and the explosion happened in a wide-open urban environment, the debris from the vehicle was much easier to find and recover, and the car was in a much better condition.

As a result I was able, within a few days, to give the police a preliminary view and was subsequently able to re-create the bombs in good detail. The similarities between the two devices were unmistakable, suggesting the same individual or individuals had assembled both.

My investigation began with an examination of the exterior and interior of both cars, followed by the removal of all the internal fixtures, and then, using an industrial vacuum cleaner with clean bags, extracting every last item from each car, which afterwards we went through particle by particle. Alongside this we examined all the debris from both scenes in the same detail.

To start with, the questions about the exact nature of the explosive force continued to mount. This was not least because I found traces of RDX high explosive, an ingredient in plastic explosive also known as Royal Demolition explosive or cyclonite, on both cars but especially on the VW. Swab tests on that vehicle produced findings of RDX in micrograms where you would normally expect nanograms after a detonation – traces that were one thousand times smaller. RDX is widely used in military or industrial applications and here it should have produced the shearing forces on the bodywork that I described earlier. Something didn't add up.

But as we began to reassemble in plan form the hundreds of disparate pieces, I started to understand why the symptoms in this case did not match the causes. The bombmaker had used small car fire extinguishers – remember the piece of red metal I had spotted on the track in Wiltshire? Well, similar pieces had been found in the debris in Bristol. He or she had filled these with RDX but had been either unable to find a proper detonator or did not realise one was required. Plastic explosive like RDX needs a shockwave to detonate it, normally created by the ignition of a much more sensitive – and thus dangerous – compound, usually stimulated by either friction, a spark, a flame or a mild shock. A good example of a detonator compound is lead azide, a highly sensitive material that is usually handled and stored underwater in insulated rubber containers.

After weeks of work, I was able to show that a cap had been attached to the top of the extinguishers in both bombs. This had been filled with gunpowder, probably sourced from fireworks, and into which the filament of a car light bulb had been inserted. When the light came on, it ignited the gunpowder, which then set fire to the RDX, which, in its confinement, exploded but not at the high intensity it was designed for. This was what we termed an 'inefficient detonation'. It was more like what we would expect to find in 'low explosive' – an example being fireworks – with a reaction speed of around 2,000 metres a second as opposed to 8,000 metres a second for high explosive. It would still have produced a big bang, but the intensity of the explosion was not capable of creating the shear forces seen on Airey Neave's car, and it explained the tearing pattern on the bodywork of both the VW and the jeep.

The whole device based on the fire extinguisher was packaged in each case in a navy blue metal 'Helix' cashbox. This was attached to the cars by at least two magnets, which had been glued to the boxes. Why? Because we discovered that when left to attach on their own, the magnets tended to preferentially stick to the underside of a car rather than the box, making it difficult to position the box exactly where you wanted it. The bombers must have discovered this too. But even their careful preparation in this area was not enough to stop the magnets failing at one end of the box in the case of the Bristol bomb.

Inside the box there were two batteries, the purpose of the second of which I was never quite sure about, and an alarm clock. We managed to recover 230 pieces of the black plastic clock, together with fragments of its innards, and I showed that it had been used as a 'safe-to-arm' or 'delay-to-arming' device in both cases. This is a common tool in an improvised bomb where one of the hands of the clock is soldered to a wire, which, after a suitable time delay, connects a circuit to the detonator. This enabled the bombers to place their devices without risk of them exploding as they did so.

The only component we could not locate was what I guessed would have been some form of tilt switch, most likely one using mercury. The movement of a car would result in the mercury being displaced to a point where it connected the circuit between the alarm clock and the filament. At that time mercury tilt switches were commonly used by the IRA in car bombs and these sorts of switches were widely available in electronics stores. It was clear that the switch had worked fairly quickly in the Wiltshire attack but it had required the box to become partially detached in Bristol for the circuit to connect. Perhaps the bomb-maker did not use a tilt switch at all and just relied on the clock to arm and connect the device? But given that both were apparently activated by a sharp movement, when the vehicle was being driven, I considered this unlikely.

I assembled a dummy of the device and noted all the correlations between the two. An identical cashbox, fire-extinguisher and clock, with similar batteries and magnets, plus identical multi-stranded and single-stranded wiring. They both utilized the same high-explosive charge containing RDX and lithium (suggesting a British form of plastic explosive) and both devices left unusually high post-explosive residues on the bodywork of the cars. The combined weight of the components in each case was very similar.

Given the amount of evidence we had – I was also careful to preserve any sections of material that might contain fingerprint evidence – it was extremely disappointing that no one was ever charged with these attacks, both of which I had no doubt could have led to loss of life. It was an early lesson for me that forensic work could not solve crimes on its own. The police did track down a vendor of magnets who recalled selling a large number to an individual – suggesting more attacks may have been planned – but that person was never traced. It may well be that the serious injuries inflicted on John Cupper, a consequence of the Bristol bombing that was unintended by its perpetrator, deterred whoever it was from mounting further attacks of this nature.

It had been an interesting first encounter with car bombs for me and we subsequently used this case in briefings to staff and security personnel. In my final years in charge at the FEL I often used it to remind people to keep an open mind when examining a scene and to remain curious at all times about what you were looking at and hearing from witnesses or victims. It is all too easy to spend hundreds of hours solving one individual thread after another but then fail to see how they all come together – and, of course, sometimes you never get the complete answer that you are striving for.

In this case I have often thought through again why Mrs Baskerville so confidently talked of hearing a whooshing sound or whump! but not a bang. Even given an apparent low-explosive device, most people would have described a bang.

Many years later I came to the conclusion that there would indeed have been a very loud bang when the device activated. This would almost certainly have stunned her and left her in a state of shock and may have momentarily caused her to lose consciousness. When the bomb detonated it cut the fuel line in the jeep, allowing petrol to pour out on to metal surfaces being heated by the explosion. Within a few seconds this would have then ignited, creating the sound that she recalled and prompting her to get out of the jeep as fast as she could.

4

A half-Dutch Rocker

You might expect a future forensic explosives expert to have spent his childhood fascinated by – or even making – bombs or perhaps fireworks. But I cannot point to anything as logical as that in my life.

In fact, I was always interested by mechanical things – making stuff and fixing things. First it was woodwork and then I graduated to bicycles before devoting much of my energies as a teenager, and budding Rocker, to fixing motorbikes and scooters . . . and exercising my reckless streak by finding ways to make them go faster.

I had no artistic bent at all. I couldn't draw for the life of me. But I loved mechanical and technical drawing and at school my uncertain path, which drove me close to breakdown at one point, led me in the direction of sciences and organic chemistry, a discipline where my struggles with maths would not hold me back.

The biggest personality in my childhood was my father, who became a policeman, and with whom I had an ambivalent relationship at best. He was a forceful individual who was always right and you argued with him at your peril. But he did instil in me an understanding of the rule of law and, over the years, I heard enough stories about what happened to those who broke it to reach firm conclusions about the parameters under which I would live my life.

I was born in May 1953 in Pembury Hospital in Kent, the second of four children and the first son of Brian Todd, then a geography and PE teacher at a secondary school in the town of Westerham. A couple of years after my birth he decided that his future lay with the police, partly because, by that route, he would qualify for a 'police house', and so our lives were changed from that moment on.

We moved to Orpington, in the outer suburbs of south-east London, and lived in a semi, in a row of ten police houses, with neighbours whose fathers were sergeants and constables in the Met, just like my own. But we were a little bit different from the other families, even if Constable Brian Todd did his best to conceal that fact.

My mother was Dutch, and a quieter, calmer, more tolerant soul than my father, who grew ever more authoritarian and inflexible as his life and career moulded him. Maria Frederika – known to us as Mies – had been brought up in the small Dutch town of Emmen, close to the German border. The daughter of a pastry chef who ran his own bakery business, she met my father at a sporting exchange in Manchester when they were both still in their late teens.

These were international get-togethers that were popular in the post-war years and were developed as a means of broadening young peoples' horizons. Mum was playing tennis at the meeting while Dad was into cycling. Somehow their paths crossed and a relationship began, which blossomed into marriage in 1950. I came along after my sister, Sue.

The interesting thing about my mum was how quickly and thoroughly she assimilated into British life, to the point where almost no one knew she was Dutch. But this wasn't entirely a voluntary or even organic process; my father did not like her Dutch accent and insisted, for example, that she speak flawless English. If he heard her talking with even a hint of her natural intonation, he would lecture her on how she should speak.

When I was eighteen, the extent to which Mum had learned to disguise her natural accent was brought home to all of us when she was required to make a short speech at the masonic lodge in Camberwell, where my father – by then a sergeant in the Met – was serving as master. Mum was terrified and, as she began talking, she did so without the veneer of English intonation that she had so assiduously acquired. We were all astonished to hear her speaking just as she must have done when she first met Dad back in the late 1940s.

Despite his campaign to Anglicise my mother, my Dutch family and background were an important part of my childhood. Both my two sisters and I – Gwen followed me – each spent six months living with our grandparents in Emmer-Compascuum and going to school in Holland, where we learnt fluent Dutch. It was an unregimented and relaxed approach to life in Holland, and I settled in easily with Oma and Opa and my Uncle Rob. Even today, when it comes to things like the World Cup, I support England first but if, and when, they have been knocked out, the Netherlands is always my second choice.

As a young boy I guess I had what you might call a happy childhood. I was quite a nervous kid, shy and introspective, never wanting to push myself forward, a trait which has stayed with me throughout my life. During my primary school years, I would kick around at home and with friends in the street. There was one boy whose father was into carpentry and in his shed in the back garden he had all the tools. We would go in there and build all sorts of things together, including a go-kart, which we would race down the street – I still have the scar on my chin from crashing it – and a crossbow.

But much of the time not a lot happened. I used to love reading adventure books like *The Famous Five*, *Treasure Island* and *The Adventurous Four*, but I can also remember sitting at home, staring out of my bedroom window across the rooftops of south London, wondering why adventures always seemed to happen to everyone else but me.

A half-Dutch Rocker

At school I sometimes earned the wrong sort of attention and suffered what would be regarded these days as low-level bullying of a kind that quiet kids sometimes seem to attract. One or two classmates regularly niggled away at me and one boy took it further with occasional physical attacks. Then, one day – and I'm still not sure where the impulse came from – I decided this particular tormentor should be taught a lesson. I clouted him hard enough to knock him to the ground, surprising both him and me in equal measure. I stood over him thinking: 'Oh my God, what's he going to do now?', fearing severe retribution. But, actually, I learnt a lesson that day to stand up for myself, because, instead of another onslaught, I seemed to have earned that kid's grudging respect.

After passing the eleven-plus, I moved from my local primary school to Bromley Grammar and it was at this point that a decision was taken that would have big consequences for me and would, in many ways, shape my entire development from then on. I had done quite well in the eleven-plus and so the school was keen for me to go into the top stream in the second year and take my O-levels a year early.

My father was all for it but my mother was more cautious. With perhaps more of an understanding of what was at stake for me personally, she spent time discussing it with the school. But eventually a decision was taken and I had to live with the consequences. While I could have sailed through schooling doing well in the lower stream, I was now condemned to a constant struggle to keep up. Almost from that moment on I had the sense that I was swimming against a tide and making no headway, just trying to keep my head above water.

When I look back I see a young boy fighting a completely needless battle and I genuinely think I came close to what we would now call a nervous breakdown as a result of the constant stress to keep up. It all became too much during my O-level year, when I passed five or six of them at the age of fifteen. But the effort of will to achieve all that left me burnt out and, from then on, I started to rebel against the self-discipline and the weight of work I had had to contend with. Until then I hadn't questioned it; now I was a young teenager in the first generation of modern British teenagers in the mid-1960s, and I could see that I had lost any sense of enjoyment in life and I wanted it back.

I stopped worrying about school and started to get into music – The Stones, and later Black Sabbath, Pink Floyd and The Who – while, at the same time, I graduated from tinkering around with pushbikes to motorbikes and scooters. My passion for speed, which in later life would manifest itself in a love of cars and driving fast, had taken hold.

I may have been shy, but I had grown into quite a wilful individual. If I wanted something, nothing was going to stop me achieving it – not even my father. I saved my pocket money from my paper round, and from working for the local butcher, delivering his wares on a big old bicycle with a ball-killer of a saddle, so that I could buy my first motorbike.

But my father was having none of it. While my elder sister had already started to have pitched battles with him on almost every idea or rule he tried to lay down, from what she wore to what he said about the big political questions of the day, I chose a more nuanced path. If I disagreed with him – which I did on many things – I didn't engage in pointless argument but instead just quietly carried on without allowing matters to deteriorate into open conflict.

I told him quietly but firmly one day that I was getting a motorbike and that was the end of it. He could see I was determined and came up with a solution that he thought would nip this apparent new hobby of mine in the bud. In the garage he had an old Lambretta scooter that a friend of his had confidently informed him was a heap of scrap.

'You can have that,' he said, 'if you can get it to work.'

While he had no idea about mechanical things and believed unquestioningly in what he had been told, I saw the opportunity to get *motorised* – it wasn't a motorbike but it had two wheels and an engine, so it would do. Together with a couple of friends from school, we got to work and sorted the scooter out – it needed little more than a new clutch and new jets in the carburettor – and I was launched.

On my red-and-white Lambretta, I passed my test and was on the road and soon entering the half-world of Britain's then raging motorbike and scooter counter-culture. At that stage Sue was going out with a Rocker – a guy she would eventually marry – and, as a sixteen-year-old who hated the idea of rules and regulations, I decided I would become one too.

While the Mods were all precision – smart hair-dos and parkas – the Rockers were my kind of people: free spirits, scruffy and also known as 'greasers' or 'the great unwashed'. I loved being part of that scene and so dressed like a Rocker, scruffy with a plastic 'leather effect' jacket. I was a bit young to join in, but watched from the fringes as the motorbike versus scooter skirmishes of Orpington were waged between the Rockers, based at Devito's café in the high street, and the Mods at the Wimpy Bar. At the same time my musical tastes broadened as I added Genesis, King Crimson, Barclay James Harvest, Mountain and Led Zeppelin to my growing record collection.

At school things went from bad to worse. I had stopped caring about my performance in class and it culminated in me failing all my A-levels – zoology, botany, chemistry and physics – which, looking back, I am sure I was quite capable of passing. The upshot was that I had to stay on and do them all over again, reversing the disastrous decision six years earlier for me to skip a year. On my second attempt I managed to pass chemistry and zoology.

On the road, meanwhile, I had traded up my father's old Lambretta to a D-Type model of the same marque, which was black and faster – 60mph tops. I loved the speed and managing the risk. I never had a serious crash but I knew people who were injured and one or two who died in those heady years when we enjoyed riding together in south London. After the D-Type I graduated to my first motorbike, a Honda 250, and then got into cars.

I had no real idea of what I wanted to do. I thought about becoming a doctor but my A-level performance put paid to that. I was interested in engineering but my Achilles heel at maths made that an unlikely avenue. Another option was working in a hospital pathology lab. With that thought in mind, I applied to the Polytechnic of Central London to study biochemistry and physiology, starting in the autumn of 1971.

I was a proper student of the day – long hair, flared jeans and the owner of a series of beaten-up old cars that I managed to get roadworthy. I would buy them at the second-hand car auctions in Dalston in east London and do them up. I would change them every six months, graduating from an early Fiat 124 to an altogether more stylish Triumph TR6.

I never did drugs, preferring a pint in the pub. I loved living in halls of residence in the centre of London – the first was right opposite Madame Tussauds on the Marylebone Road – and I took full advantage of the opportunity to go to as many gigs as I could. Among the ones I remember most were Mountain and then Barclay James Harvest at the Rainbow, Led Zeppelin at Fairfield Halls in Croydon and, later, Pink Floyd at the Hammersmith Odeon.

My heroes? In those days I was a great admirer of David Gilmour of the Floyd and Pete Townshend of The Who, even though the latter had always had a bit of a reputation as a Mod band. I was never an extremist politically, but was aware of what was going on in a world in which the news was dominated by reports from Vietnam abroad and the Troubles in Northern Ireland closer to home.

I was part of a generation of British and American youth who wanted to change the world but never quite managed it. We wanted peace and love instead of war and we set out to challenge the old notions of what was right and wrong, how society should be run, how we should work, dress and love, and we almost got it right. But it seems to me that we let it slip through our fingers – the road to our new world has never quite reached its destination and our early idealism has gradually been overtaken by the inevitable cynicism of middle age.

I graduated in 1974, the proud possessor of a BSc in biochemistry and physiology – third class honours – a qualification recognised by London University as a so-called 'external degree'. Then I set off with a friend on a month-long Greyhound bus tour of America, where we completed a great circle from New York out to LA and back. On my return, I worked in an engineering factory, turning widgets on a lathe as I recall, and then spent a few months working for another friend who was making his living as an electrician, rewiring houses and a small factory.

All the while I was applying for various laboratory positions, particularly in hospitals or biochemistry labs, and then one day I spotted an ad for a job with the Health and Safety Executive (HSE).

5

From health and safety to the study
of bombs

I know what you're thinking. The Health and Safety
Executive – how boring is that? Well, yes and no. Actually, some of the work *is* comparatively dull and, as part
of the civil service, the HSE has sometimes been less
efficient than it might have been, but I always thought
of it as an organisation that fulfils a useful function in
society. In recent years the wider concept of health and
safety, and occasional absurd restrictions on how we live
or work proposed in its name and highlighted by the press,
has given the industry a bad name. But the HSE itself has
continued to do what it was set up to do – enforce the
Health and Safety at Work Act 1974.

I joined in mid-1975 and was based at the headquarters at Staples Corner in London as a scientific officer on
a salary of £2,000 a year. I was assigned to a laboratory
with a mass spectrometer, working on a series of air quality
surveys to detect the possible presence of harmful carcino-
gens in factories. Among our main targets were coke ovens,

which heated coal to make smokeless fuel, aluminium factories where coke was used to smelt ore to produce aluminium, and tyre factories in which the process of curing rubber produced toxic fumes.

We would turn up and strap small air sampler devices on to the arms of workers in these factories and then follow them around, mapping where they were at various times during the manufacturing process. Then we would collect up the samples and take them back to the lab, where my job was to do the chemistry to analyse what we had found and then report that to the HSE inspector in charge of the programme. In many cases we were able to order that breathing equipment or other protective measures be introduced to protect workers. It was rewarding work because I could see we were making a difference to people's lives and to their health, and I spent five years working mainly in heavy industry on these sorts of projects.

A couple of years into my time at Staples Corner, I bumped into the woman who would become my wife. Vanessa Parbury was a bubbly, vivacious and extroverted character – the polar opposite to me – and attractive too, with long dark hair and green eyes. She had been looking for a job in teaching but had taken a better paid position with the HSE, running the organisation's typing pool in what were the last years before computerisation.

I can't remember our first encounter – did our eyes lock on to each other during a particularly uninteresting meeting or did we talk one day at the staff bar over a pint at lunchtime? Either way, we hit it off immediately. I think she found me possibly slightly less superficial than other men she had met. Vanessa was from Plymouth, where her father had been an officer in the Royal Navy. She and her three sisters were brought up in a certain style and in a family that, on her father's side, traced its origins back to the lower nobility of the 1300s. On her mother's side, there had been money from the Lagonda car business, which had been co-founded by Vanessa's grandfather.

I got on extremely well with my father-in-law to be, who had moved on from a life at sea to selling insurance. The same could not be said of my future mother-in-law, who was angry with a world that had deposited her in a rented flat in Plymouth, which was certainly not how she had imagined her life would pan out. I wasn't the only one who found her difficult, because Vanessa did too.

At that time I was living a bachelor existence with two friends in a rented three-bedroom flat in east London, which Vanessa, understandably, found hard to cope with. It was *Men Behaving Badly* ahead of its time and the domestic arrangements were rough, to put it mildly. To give you an idea, we chucked out all the cutlery and most of the pots and pans, with the exception of one or two odds and sods and one fork, knife and spoon each – all in the cause of reducing the washing-up to an absolute minimum.

From health and safety to the study of bombs

In some ways life was good, but I was earning next to nothing and there was no chance of promotion. I couldn't see how I was ever going to buy a house or get ahead at work. It was at this stage in my life that I made an error of judgment that taught me once and for all to stay on the straight and narrow.

I had a friend from my Rocker days who had always straddled the fence between the law-abiding world I had grown up in and the south London criminal underworld. Over the years I had come to know some of Jake's friends who were involved in crime and who we would meet socially from time to time. I knew how they made their living – burglaries and occasional robberies. I wasn't part of it, but I was a friend of Jake's, so I was accepted and we would talk sport, cars and women. They were rough and flawed, certainly, but I had no problem spending time with them.

So when Jake invited me to meet another of his criminal associates, I was not unduly concerned. Knowing I was working as a chemist by this time, he had asked me if I knew anything about red diesel – and specifically if I knew how to take out the red colouring. This is fuel that is used in farm vehicles and plant machinery that is not available on public roads and is not taxed at the same rate as road diesel. To distinguish it from the fuel used on roads, it has a red dye added, and roadside checks are commonly made on commercial vehicles to make sure they are not cheating the system.

Foolishly I had told Jake I could probably come up with a way of removing the dye and it was this that his associate was interested in.

'Look, I think I know how this can be done, but I am not going to get involved,' I said.

'Don't you worry,' Jake replied. 'This guy has heard about what can be done – he just wants to hear it from you and make sure no one is taking him for ride.'

All of which led to a big mistake on my part and a valuable lesson about who I wanted to be. I found myself sitting in a pub somewhere in southeast London, facing a man I had assumed would be just like the others. But he wasn't. He was entirely different and I sensed it almost as soon as I sat down.

After a few pleasantries he asked me about my work, and then moved straight on to red diesel. It was all very polite, but he just oozed evil and menace. Perhaps it was the eyes; it seemed there was something essentially human missing, and I remember feeling like I was being inspected for possible use, as if by an alien who had taken on human form. I had never experienced anyone like this before, nor have I, this close up, ever since.

I answered his questions then hurriedly tried to empha-sise that, though simple in principle, to remove dye at scale would be much more complicated and require chemical engineering expertise that I did not have. I just wanted to get away from there as fast and as far as I could.

Afterwards, I told Jake that he was on his own; I wanted nothing to do with this scheme or that man ever again – and I never did. To his credit, Jake told me he understood what I was saying – perhaps he also sensed something of what I had – and he never raised it again. But it taught me something of the nature of criminality and where it can lead. It also crystallised in my mind that law breaking is largely a choice, and 'straddling the fence', for me at least, was not an option. Sooner or later I would have to choose and that time was now; I would have no more contact with anyone involved in crime, or entertain any kind of unlawful enterprise.

After five years in the job at HSE, I got itchy feet and put in my resignation letter. I wanted a new challenge and couldn't see where that was coming from. However, unbeknown to me, a reorganisation of the way the HSE worked was underway and the plan was to set up a series of local labs around the country, one of which was based in East Grinstead in West Sussex. My boss encouraged me to accept a position there, a move sweetened by the offer of being able to move at public expense, which meant I would qualify for a series of allowances.

So Vanessa and I – we were living together by then – packed up and left London for a job that was much more varied than the work I had been doing at Staples Corner, even if I remained at the rank of scientific officer. With the help of the money offered to assist our move, we managed to buy a tiny, two-bedroomed Victorian cottage in the village of Edenbridge in Kent, from where I could commute to work. Vanessa found a job of her own as a cashier in a bank on Edenbridge High Street and, a year after arriving, we tied the knot with a wedding at our local church, attended by a handful of friends and family. We followed it with a one-night honeymoon at a hotel in Croydon.

At the new lab I did more work on noxious materials – dust in brickworks, fumes in paint manufacturing plants, but also other elements of safety at work, such as measuring noise levels in a paper mill and assessing the effectiveness of safety guards on big cutting and pressing machinery in various factories.

It was at this stage that I also got the chance to contribute to some early computer modelling of major hazard installations and what would happen if poisonous or unstable gasses escaped during a failure of tanks or piping. This was work that I would later draw on when giving evidence about the IRA bombing of a gasworks in Warrington in Cheshire.

I found this sort of thing fascinating. We would examine what would happen if, say, a large tank of chlorine gas started to leak. We looked at various rates of leakage, how clouds of gas would form and spread depending on the chemicals involved and the influence of wind and moisture on how the gas would behave. By today's standards we were working on very simple computers, but it felt cutting edge at the time. My job was to write programs to collate all the information needed to put into the mainframe so that it could run an analysis that would be useful to the emergency services responding to incidents of this sort.

Four years after we arrived in Edenbridge, Vanessa gave birth to Andrew and we decided almost immediately that we would have to move to a bigger house. Within a few months we had sold up and moved to Southborough, between Tonbridge and Tunbridge Wells, where we bought an Edwardian semi that remained the family home for years. By the time Andrew arrived, I had started to get that five-year itch again and was thinking of moving on from the HSE.

It was at this point that I spotted an internal civil-service memo advertising for applications for something called the Forensic Explosives Laboratory, an organisation I had never heard of. I was intrigued. The ad described performing chemical analysis of explosives and working in a laboratory for the police and security community. This sounded very interesting indeed and I noticed that the job was based just down the road from Orpington. I had driven past Fort Halstead thousands of times when it was still known as the Royal Armaments Research and Defence Establishment.

EXPLOSIVE

I applied and was surprised to be asked for what was described as an 'informal interview'. I assumed this would be a preliminary chat to see if I was suitable and then I would be asked back if they thought I had a chance. I put on a suit and went to the Fort and met Kevin Henderson (not his real name), then the head of casework at the FEL. We had a very relaxed discussion during which he asked about the work I had been doing at the HSE and my studies at college. Afterwards I was shown around the various labs and machines – mass spectrometers, gas chromatographs, infrared spectrometers, ultraviolet spectrometers, liquid chromatography machines etc.

We also toured the stores and exhibits and I was shown some of the debris from the bombing of the Grand Hotel in Brighton, an IRA 'spectacular' three years earlier in 1984 that had killed five people and injured thirty-one others during the Tory Party conference, which I remembered all too clearly from news reports at the time. I began to realise that this place was all about bombs, the illegal use of explosives and trying to work out what had been used and by whom. That meant I would be working in a highly sensitive and secretive environment and would be part of Britain's legal and defence response to IRA terrorism and other forms of violent protest involving explosives. It felt exciting and daunting all at once.

I told Henderson that I was worried I might be wasting

his time. I knew nothing about explosives, I explained, and I was not a forensic scientist.

He seemed comfortable with that.

'Don't worry,' he said, laughing. 'Very few people know much about explosives or bombs when they come here. We will teach you all of that – you are an analytical chemist and a lot of what you might do will be in that area and we will teach you the rest.'

I heard nothing for six weeks and assumed I was not going to be asked back for a second interview. I had put it out of my mind and was mulling over whether to move with the HSE as the organisation decamped to its new headquarters in Sheffield. Then a letter arrived from the FEL that I assumed was going to tell me I had been rejected. I opened it almost absent-mindedly and discovered I had been offered a job as a trainee case officer in the Forensics Explosives Laboratory.

My life would never be the same again.

6

Thailand – when explosive forensic science is made impossible

It was the Whitsun Bank Holiday in 1991, just under a year after the animal rights car bombing case had taken me to Wiltshire, and I was the on-call duty chemist at the FEL.

I was at home with Andrew, who was then seven, while Vanessa went off to Birmingham to stay with her sister. We had agreed that if I had to pop into the lab for any reason – perhaps to conduct some tests on samples that came in over the holiday – then Andrew could go to our neighbours, who had a boy of the same age.

These arrangements did not cover the eventuality of me hopping on a flight to Bangkok four hours after being called by Norman Barraclough (not his real name), the head of the lab.

'Cliff, it's Norman Barraclough,' he told me, with an urgency that suggested something serious was up.

'Oh, hello, Norman, yes, how are –'

'Look, I need to you to go to Thailand.'

'What?

Thailand – when forensic science is made impossible

'Thailand, Bangkok . . . have you been following the news?'

'Err, well, yes, but . . .'

'Okay, so yesterday a passenger jet operated by the Austrian carrier Lauda Air – the one owned by the racing driver – suddenly and inexplicably crashed from cruising altitude shortly after take-off from Bangkok for Vienna.'

'OK, yeah, now you mention it . . .'

'The thing is, there is already a good deal of speculation that it might have been blown up and Lloyd's of London, who insure the plane, want our view on it. So pack a few things and be ready in half an hour. A car is coming to pick you up – your flight from Heathrow is in four hours' time.'

Jesus! To say that I was feeling out of my depth once again would be a massive understatement.

'I presume everyone was killed, then?' I offered.

'Yes, all 213 passengers and ten crew – the plane came down in dense forest not far from the Thai–Burmese border. You'll be there in 24 hours alongside Ian Leadsome from Lloyd's, who will be in charge, and Kevin Henderson and Keith Vaughn [not their real names].'

'I'm supposed to be looking after my son this weekend because my wife has gone to Birmingham,' I said, feeling rather ridiculous about injecting the mundane details of domestic life into what was both a tragic situation and a major professional opportunity.

'Well, you'll just have to find a way round that, I'm afraid. Right-oh, Cliff. Take care, good luck, see what you can find.'

'Yes . . . Okay, thanks, Norman. I'll do my best.'

I put the phone down and stood in the hallway of our home, stunned by what I had heard and what I was now going to be expected to do. It wasn't just that I'd barely travelled outside Europe, apart from the Greyhound tour of the States after I graduated, it was more that I was still quite a junior case officer and I had never imagined my responsibilities might include conducting forensic work in Asia.

Andrew was running around in the garden, pretending he was driving a car. I needed a solution to his care . . . and now.

I called our neighbour and told them that something completely unexpected had cropped up. Would they very much mind having Andrew to stay for a couple of nights? I couldn't phone Vanessa and ask her to come back because she was still out and about in Birmingham with her sister – they had gone to lunch and then out shopping. In an age before mobile phones were widely available, there was no way to contact her before I left for Heathrow.

They assured me that it was no problem, that they would take Andrew until Vanessa came back from Birmingham. Andrew was delighted; sleepovers were always good, and he thought this whole episode was really cool – a big limo with several men in, coming and whisking his dad away to some foreign country. But he could tell I was feeling nervous about what lay ahead. He always liked soft toys, and he suddenly disappeared into his bedroom and emerged with a small teddy. He told me gravely that this was Nog, and that I should take him with me, as he would look after me on my travels.

That night I sat up for most of the long flight to Bang-kok, thinking about what might be ahead of us in the coming days. This was an international incident that was still very much in the news and we were going to the scene. While Wiltshire had been my first car bomb, this was going to be my first passenger jet crash and it might have been caused by a bomb; I felt again that mixture of excitement and stage fright that I experienced every time I was sent to a new scene for the FEL.

I wondered what we would find there. We knew the plane had come down in woodland. Was it in one piece? Would there be bodies hanging in the trees? I imagined the scene would be deserted and in a wild place where we could examine everything in forensically pristine condition. We knew from our collective experience of Lockerbie that a disciplined and systematic approach to crash debris and the personal effects of passengers and crew was vital if reliable conclusions were to be reached and key pieces of evidence were to be identified and saved. But this would be an assignment that would teach me key lessons about the limits of forensic work and the critical importance of a properly preserved and protected scene.

I was very much the junior member of the party, ready to do what I was told. Leadsome, short in stature but brimful of energy, was a senior loss adjuster and aircraft crash investigator for Lloyd's, who were effectively our clients in this case and were paying for the trip. When accidents like this happened, Lloyd's responded with impressive speed. In this case the Boeing 767-300ER, which was less than two years old and was named *Mozart*, was covered by two underwriters. One was a 'war risk' group and the other an 'all risk' group, which covered everything other than an act of war or sabotage, including a terrorist bombing. When the plane came down, the initial estimate for its total loss was around £40 million. Since it was not clear which underwriting syndicate was responsible for the pay-out, they had both stumped up £20 million and, once it had been established who was liable, that group would then pay back the other party. But Leadsome was in a rush to reach a conclusion because whichever syndicate was liable was also required to pay interest on the half sum put up by the other party, so a decision needed to be made and quickly.

Henderson, meanwhile, who wore a beard but no moustache, had been in charge of casework when I joined the FEL but had since moved to another department at the

Thailand – when forensic science is made impossible

Fort, where he was responsible for all the kit used by military bomb disposal officers. He had prior experience of air crash investigation, having been at the scene of Lockerbie on day one. Vaughn, a down-to-earth and friendly companion on the trip, was a metallurgist at the Fort who was a specialist at looking for and identifying micro-cratering in metals associated with explosions. Like Henderson, he had done a fair amount of work on Lockerbie.

If going abroad to work at the scene of a major air crash was a shock, so was the way we travelled. We had been picked up by a smart, chauffeur-driven Mercedes, which had initially dropped by the Fort. There I grabbed anything I thought I might need – gloves, forensic white suits, swab kits – before we were whisked off to Heathrow. Then it was fast track through security to the plane and business-class seats to Bangkok International.

The next morning we hit the ground running. I barely got any feel for the heat and humidity because we went from arrivals straight into an air-conditioned limo and then made our way through the chaotic and largely gridlocked streets of the Thai capital to the Shangri-La hotel, no less. When I got to my room, I called Vanessa, nearly a day after she had caught a train to Birmingham. Our neighbours had phoned through to her sister's that evening, so she already knew that Andrew was safely looked after, but almost nothing else – just that I was halfway round the world at some plane crash, so she was still understandably anxious.

EXPLOSIVE

Although I could not say exactly when I would be back –
a few days at most, I thought – I was able to reassure her
I was perfectly safe and would be in touch when I could.

I had only had a few minutes to make the call because
we went straight into a massive meeting that the Thai
authorities were staging in the conference room of a hotel
nearby. It was then that I realised that we were most definitely not alone. Experts in their fields had been flying in
from all over the world in response to the tragedy that was
Lauda Air Flight 004. (Niki Lauda himself had already
gone to the crash site and would later attend the funerals
of twenty-three of the victims in Bangkok).

In addition to our small party, there were people from
Boeing, from Lauda Air, from the Austrian government,
from the National Transportation Safety Board – the
American version of our Air Accident Investigation Branch
– plus diplomats from some of the other affected countries,
particularly Hong Kong, which had had fifty-two passengers on the plane, and then a range of Thai officials from
the police, army and air force. The object was to welcome
us all – and the diplomatic niceties went on and on – and
then try to work out who needed what assistance and
when.

Our goal was to get to the crash site, about 65 miles
northwest of Bangkok, as soon as possible, and we managed to enlist the good offices of the Thai military, who
organised a helicopter to take us the following morning.

Thailand – when forensic science is made impossible

This was something else; helicoptering across Thailand to try to nail the people who may have brought this jet down.

The theory that a bomb might have been involved was being widely speculated upon in the world's press because it was very unusual for a plane to suddenly fall out of the sky from level flight. But an Austrian-flagged jet seemed an odd target, given that the government in Vienna was not known for its foreign commitments or for particularly contentious policies that might provoke extremists to attack it. Nevertheless, the scant details about the crash still made foul play at least a possibility.

After arriving from Hong Kong, the plane had taken off from Don Mueang International Airport in Bangkok as normal, at the beginning of a thrice-weekly service to the Austrian capital. The aircraft had reached its cruising altitude at almost 30,000ft as normal but then, just 15 minutes into the flight, it came hurtling to the ground in what was the deadliest aviation disaster in Thai history and the deadliest incident involving a Boeing 767.

I was ready to join them on the helicopter trip but Leadsome decided my time would be better spent holding the fort at the hotel, while he and the other two did a preliminary survey of the main wreckage site. I was understandably disappointed to be kicking around – albeit in a five-star hotel – rather than going to the crash site and Leadsome sensed I needed something to do.

'Oh, Cliff,' he said, as we finished dinner late that night, when I was struggling to keep my eyes open. 'Look, while we are busy tomorrow, why don't you have a go at finding some large-scale maps of the crash area? That would be very useful for us in terms of trying to pinpoint exactly where the various debris clusters are. I'm sure you won't have much trouble finding a good map shop in Bangkok and the hotel will be able to help.'

'Yeah, no problem,' I said, feeling very much the B-team.

The next day, the others were full of understandable anticipation about what they might find. There was a lot of talk about Lockerbie and what had been found in Scotland that first indicated a bomb. Initially at least, the focus was almost certainly going to have to be on luggage, given the likelihood that if a device had been smuggled on to the aircraft it would have been in a suitcase in the hold. Had there been a fire on the ground? Or in mid-air? How far apart were the main wreckage sites? What condition were the sites going to be in, more than 48 hours after the crash?

I listened to them talking over breakfast, wanting so much to be part of the team that day. But when they headed off to the military airfield, I got into my first ever tuk-tuk motorised scooter and headed off to the outskirts of the city, where the concierge had confidently predicted I would find detailed maps of his homeland. The trouble

90

was – and I worked this out pretty quickly – Thailand was a military-backed regime and ordinary people were not expected to have access to highly detailed maps of rural areas of the country. I knew from the outset that my chances of finding anything of any use were going to be slim.

I sat on the narrow bench behind the driver as we threaded our way between the cars, trucks and buses, feeling the warm and humid air flowing across my face. It was delivering what I imagined (because I have no sense of smell, having been born that way – a condition called anosmia) was a mixture of food smells with diesel and petrol fumes as we ducked in and out of the traffic, heading further and further out of town.

Eventually I was dumped outside the first shop the concierge had directed me to. We were a long way from the centre of the city and I was now very much on my own and struggling to communicate with the locals. And it was hot, beyond anything I had previously known, and I could feel a headache coming on even before I had started trying to find what I was looking for.

After about half an hour of fruitless exchanges in simple English, I realised the place did not have the sort of maps I needed. I trudged out into the steam-bath atmosphere and began walking back towards the centre of the city and towards the next shop that had been circled on my map by the concierge. After lots of pointing at a map of Thailand on the wall of the shop – and showing the proprietor the Thai words for Suphan Buri Province, where the plane had come down – I realised he too had nothing of any use.

I was beginning to think this was indeed a hopeless quest – trying to find the equivalent of a 2½-inch scale OS map of an obscure area of hilly, heavily-forested country near the Thai–Burmese border, without being able to speak the local language or explain why I needed the maps. This was certainly not what I had envisaged I would be doing on this trip when we left London the day before, and I couldn't help but feel frustrated.

I walked on to the third shop on my list and got nowhere there either. There was one more address to check out, but by then I'd almost had enough. I was sweating profusely. My thick cotton shirt was soaked through and my head was starting to pound as dehydration kicked in. I managed to find the fourth map shop and was amazed to find that the helpful owner not only spoke quite a bit of English but also had an extraordinary range of detailed maps. I couldn't believe it. I felt so relieved. I would be able to calmly offer Leadsome exactly what he had asked for and make it look like it had been no sweat from the start.

I paid for the maps and stepped back into the furnace outside and nearly collapsed. Little did I know it but I was now dangerously dehydrated, having drunk nothing since breakfast and eaten nothing. I started to ramble along the busy street, stumbling and feeling my vision narrowing. It began to dawn on me that I was about to pass out. What a disastrous start to my 'foreign career' as a forensic scientist with the FEL that would have been, I thought.

I quickly forgot about the hotel. I needed water and quick. I saw the entrance to a small mall on the other side of the street and headed straight for it. Walking through the sliding doors, I entered an ice-cool world of air-conditioned peace and quiet. I slumped down at a table in a small café and ordered one glass of water after another, and then a Coke. I sat there for nearly an hour gathering my strength; talk about an Englishman abroad . . .

That night I was eager to catch up with the others and find out what they had seen. The mood was gloomy, which was not unexpected given the nature of our assignment. But it wasn't the death and destruction that was preying on Leadsome's mind and on Henderson's and Vaughn's, but what they had seen at the main wreckage site. To their astonishment and dismay, there were hundreds of people swarming all over it, scavenging for whatever they could find either from the remains of the plane itself or from the personal effects of the passengers and crew.

'I couldn't believe my eyes – this is going to be a real struggle,' summarised Leadsome tersely. 'We are going to be working in a completely anarchic setting where just about everything will have been moved or picked up or nicked. Let's just hope we can see enough to still be able to come to some sensible conclusions.'

We then spent some time poring over the maps, marking the grid co-ordinates of the main debris fields and getting a sense of exactly where the crash had happened. This was all the more important because the following day a helicopter would not be available; we would be travelling by four-wheel jeep.

We left at 4.30 a.m. to begin the four-hour journey northwest from Bangkok. I sat in the back noting the case of water bottles alongside me that Henderson had organised. These guys know what they are doing out here, I thought. I was keen to get going and to make my contribution. I felt sure we could still do some effective work, despite the invasion of the crash site.

The first part of the journey was straightforward and was largely on tarmacked roads. But the last hour became a real ordeal as we headed off on to rough tracks in the forest, with the three of us now joined by a forest ranger to guide us to the site. What with all our gear, and the vehicle bumping and rolling, it was hardly business class.

When we finally got out and stretched our legs, the heat felt even more intense than it had been during my map-hunting expedition in Bangkok. Out here it was oppressive and the mosquitoes were quickly in attendance. We sprayed ourselves with insect repellent from top to bottom and tucked our trousers into our socks as the ranger beckoned us forward along a track cutting straight into bamboo and trees.

On the horizon were low wooded peaks. The place was very quiet, apart from the low hum of insects and the call of the birds. There was no sign of agriculture or settlement. This was not the tourist Thailand that we are familiar with from holiday brochures today; it was deep in the heart of nowhere, as far as I was concerned, and it made me think of Vietnam. Imagine all this – the insects (I also conjured up images of snakes, lizards and scorpions) *and* the Vietcong trying to kill you with booby traps and ambushes. I could see just what a hellish time American troops must have had trying to patrol in country like this.

After a short while the ranger stopped and pointed downwards to his right. We all gathered to peer down the hillside. I guessed this would be my first glimpse of what I had come to Thailand to see: the remains of a modern jet airliner lying broken, twisted and smashed in a remote corner of forest, thousands of miles from its destination on the edge of the Austrian Alps.

I took a deep breath and peered down with the others. There at the bottom of a steep ravine we could see the front section of the aircraft. The nose and cockpit were clearly visible, together with quite a large area of fuselage behind it. I had never seen anything like it before and stood transfixed, imagining how this familiar shape had managed to end up in that state and in that place.

EXPLOSIVE

One of the others mentioned that all the bodies had been retrieved from the crash sites except for the pilot – the American captain of Flight 004, Thomas J. Welch – whose body was found still strapped into his seat. His was the last to be recovered because the place where the cockpit had ended up – that I was now looking at – proved the most difficult for rescue teams to get to.

'Okay, let's go,' said the ranger quietly, in English, as he waved us forward. I knew we were coming to the main crash site but I had no idea what to expect. Would the plane be largely intact, like the cockpit section, or was it just going to be a mass of twisted metal, wiring, insulation, seating and luggage?

We scrambled up quite a steep slope. I remember thinking I was probably going to be bitten by some horrible creature as I placed my hands in the undergrowth to help pull myself up. Then we came over the brow of a small hump and there before us stretched a vista I will never forget. In place of the thousands of bamboo stems and foliage that foreshortened our depth of field was a clearing made by a modern passenger jet that was later determined to have disintegrated in mid-air and may have broken the sound barrier as it came hurtling to the ground.

The impact had swept the forest away in a great swath, the size of a football pitch. In its place was a carpet of debris made up of the majority of the external and internal structure of a jet aircraft spread out on the forest floor.

Thailand – when forensic science is made impossible

There were large pieces of recognisable white fuselage, an engine and part of the undercarriage and wings, but the rest was like a rubbish heap distributed as if in some sort of weird collage.

My vision, on the flight over from London, of a remote and pristine scene, could not have been further from the reality that confronted us. Just as the team had reported the day before, the place was crawling with local people who lived in villages in the hills around and about and who had been the first to see parts of the plane coming down two days earlier. It was eerie. There were scores of people – mainly women and young men – picking up bits of metal, working their way through open suitcases, discarding things or placing them in piles for collection. But they made almost no sound.

Our ranger walked up to a group of women and explained to them who we were. Whatever he said it had an instant affect. Within a few seconds everyone had melted away back into the trees, from where they sat watching us in the shadows as we moved forward to see for ourselves what was left. I watched them bowing and putting their hands together as if to say, 'Please don't blame us. We mean no harm.'

This was a crash scene in total chaos and we had to walk in it, on it and through it – pieces of clothing, insulation, wiring, seating, carpet, aluminium sections of fuselage – it was all thrown together. I felt angry for a moment or two. How on earth were we going to find out why so many people had died here when the wreckage had been so badly disturbed? Apart from big items, like sections of fuselage or undercarriage, we knew that almost everything else had been picked up and then dropped again. There was no way of guessing how things might have looked in the moments after the plane ploughed into this dense forest floor.

We all put our disappointment to the backs of our minds and tried to do our jobs. I focused on trying to do my best, whatever the circumstances. But the state of this place shocked me.

I was tasked by Henderson to try to find bits of metal or luggage that might show signs of explosive damage – that meant looking for ragged or broken edges on sections of fuselage – or pieces of metal with signs of pitting from particles being hammered into them by the action of high explosive. I spent most of my time looking for luggage and luggage containers – again Lockerbie was in the back of all our minds and the discovery in Scotland of evidence of a bomb in a suitcase in a forward luggage container.

But what were the chances we would find that sort of thing here? We worked away in the heat and humidity, picking our way through the mess of detritus, just as the scavengers had done before us. They must have wondered what on earth we were looking for as we picked up bits of metal and held them to the light or peered at them intently for a few moments, perhaps with a magnifying glass, before dropping them again. We looked at one of the engines, but we all knew our chances of finding any evidence of a bomb in that area were virtually nil.

I had been sifting away for some hours, working my way through personal effects – clothes, books, toiletries – when I stopped in my tracks. I had spotted something that brought the reality of where we were and what we were doing right home. It was a baby's shoe lying half hidden in among broken insulation material and wiring. It was tiny, made of brown leather with a buckle and a strap, the sort toddlers everywhere wear, and the sight of it made me take a sharp intake of breath. For me, this brought the human dimension of this incident suddenly and shockingly into sharp focus. Real people of all ages and creeds had died in their hundreds here just a few hours earlier. I stepped back and joined the Thais under the trees, collecting my thoughts and trying to get my emotions back in check. There was still a job to do, and being overwhelmed by the enormity of it all was not going to help. Later the sight of an in-flight menu, no doubt offering the customers of Lauda Air a choice of chicken or beef, had a similar effect. Like the shoe, it made the human dimension all too real – this could have been people I knew and loved dying here.

We spent most of the day at the site and all of us were utterly drained by the time we got back to the jeep for the return journey to Bangkok. We had found one or two bits of metal that we thought might show fire damage. But there was not much excitement among us that we might have found something indicative of a bomb. The trouble with fire damage is it can be difficult to know if it is from a fire that might have happened in the air, or from when the plane hit the ground after it crashed. Making that distinction becomes almost impossible if materials have been moved around on the ground after the crash. Having seen how the scene had been treated, our expectations of finding anything conclusive were low.

One thing did cause a bit of excitement, however. That was the discovery by Leadsome of a Lauda Air notebook that he was convinced had come from the cockpit. It was full of handwritten notes, but what drew his attention was a hand-drawn graph, complete with upright and horizontal axes. At one point on the curve, the initials 'MCP' had been written and we all spent some time trying to work out what that could mean. Leadsome came up with the idea that the letters stood for 'Major Control Problem' and argued that it was perhaps a final message from one of the pilots and could be significant.

Later one of us came up with another idea. Perhaps MCP stood for 'Maintain Cabin Pressure'. The figure '10,000' was written next to the line on the graph. Was the pilot trying to descend to that altitude, the point at which passengers can breathe normally without oxygen? It felt like we were grasping at straws, which we undoubtedly were. We sat in the jeep in silence as we made our way back to the teeming streets of the Thai capital.

The next day we went back, and the next. We continued our search, because it took that long to get through the enormous pile of debris at that main crash site. But we were all succumbing to a feeling of hopelessness about this mission. None of us wanted to admit it openly, but it increasingly felt like a waste of time. It is hard to describe how daunting a crash site of this nature can be when it is unguarded and with no system applied to its analysis and examination. There was no one in charge, no categorisation of what had been looked at, and what had not, and after two days I was beginning to run out of energy. It felt like we were looking for something that could not be found and it was easy to start picking over the same pieces twice. That was a depressing feeling.

On day three we decided to try something different. During their helicopter flight on the first day, the other three had noticed some much smaller debris fields quite a few miles east of the main crash site. If a bomb had gone off in mid-flight, they argued, it would have produced a fine shower of small debris where it had punctured the fuselage. This would have reached the ground many miles before the main body of a plane that was travelling at 460 mph. After checking the maps with the grid references given to us by the Thai military, we set off for one of these sites, hopeful that if this tragedy was the result of an explosive charge of some sort, we might find something that at least suggested it as a possibility.

We visited a couple of sites with another ranger to guide us. But again we only found a few odds and ends – some fragments of cloth and a few bits of metal that we swabbed for explosive traces – but there was nothing that quickened our pulses.

In the end our final conclusion was that we could find no evidence of explosive involvement in the crash. That didn't mean it was completely out of the question; it was more that the conditions at the crash site made it impossible for us to ascertain if a bomb had been used. That meant, for our customer – Lloyd's insurance – the 'all risk' syndicate would have to pay up.

My own gut feeling was that we had looked conscientiously and found nothing. I found it hard to believe a bomb had brought the plane down but, at that stage, there were few other rational explanations. I wanted to see what the black boxes had to say. In the event, it turned out that the Flight Data Recorder had been almost completely destroyed in the crash, leaving investigators to focus on the Cockpit Voice Recorder and other research at the scene.

Eight months after our trip to Thailand, the full explanation for the loss of Flight 004 was published by the

Thailand – when forensic science is made impossible

Thai Air Accident Investigation Committee. In an almost unprecedented mid-air event, it was concluded that the reverse thrust function on the left-hand side of the two Pratt & Witney engines had kicked in without command, causing the plane to dive to the left and pick up speed to the point where it broke up before hitting the ground.

Reverse thrust is used in most jet airliners to slow a plane down after landing by reversing the direction that air is expelled from the engines. It's sudden deployment at cruising altitude made the airliner impossible to control and the pilots had almost no chance of rectifying the situation before it was too late. Investigators determined that a faulty electronically-controlled valve was to blame and, in the wake of the crash, a new locking device was installed on all affected aircraft, including the Boeing 767 fleet.

My own biggest take-away from this experience was comparing what I had seen in Thailand with what I had seen and heard about Lockerbie and the work the FEL had done in the aftermath of that tragedy. Lockerbie was how it should be done, from a post-crash forensics point of view, with properly-controlled, preserved and policed crash scenes; the Lauda air crash was at the opposite extreme – this was how it should *not* be done. The fact that we were not able to come to a firm conclusion one way or another on the likelihood of a bomb was one of the many inevitable consequences of the failure of the Thai authorities to police the debris fields.

EXPLOSIVE

When I got home, exhausted after our five-day trip, I presented Andrew with Nog. He had done a good job looking after me, I told him, on a journey and adventure when, for much of the time, I had felt a very long way out of my depth.

7

Coming close to eternity

It was not an instantaneous thought. More a creeping and horrifying realisation, as my mind ran through the ramifications of what I had just seen, and my blood ran cold.

What was it that had saved this man's life and saved him from being blown into so many pieces that there would have been nothing left to bury?

A speck of dust? A tiny contaminating blob of glue, invisible to the naked eye? Or perhaps a freak and equally visually undetectable manufacturing error in the production of a harmless-looking so-called 'actuating-button' that had made it stick, half in, half out?

I had barely touched it with the prong from my voltmeter and it had snapped out into its rightful position with a barely audible click. Then, when I tried to get it to sit back where I had found it, it refused to obey.

As I put the meter down, I began to realise that this had been a one-off malfunction. There was no second chance because now the switch was working perfectly. Even an almost imperceptible impact from the bomb disposal officer's investigating hand would have been enough to jolt the button into its correct position. At that point there would have been nothing to stop it completing the circuit to a detonator stuffed into 28lb of Semtex plastic explosive.

The bomb disposal officer with the Metropolitan Police who had courageously disarmed this contraption – a device that was capable of destroying a large building and killing and injuring hundreds of people inside it – had come closer to eternity than I would ever see again in all my years at the FEL.

I even wondered whether God himself was keeping an eye out for him that day as he snipped the wires to the detonator, unaware how close he was to killing himself.

I called the police liaison officer at the Fort and talked through with him what I had found. 'I think you might want to find out who the bomb disposal officer was and explain to him just how lucky he is still to be alive,' I said.

This was the summer of 1991, just a month after my trip to Thailand and shortly before I was promoted to senior case officer at the FEL. It was the start of another campaign of IRA attacks in London that targeted shops and pubs with incendiary devices. These followed a failed attempt to wipe out the Prime Minister, John Major, and his cabinet, with a mortar attack on Downing Street, and bombings of Paddington and Victoria stations. Only the Victoria attack had caused significant recent casualties, with one man killed and thirty-eight people injured.

Coming close to eternity

The station bombs came with coded warnings. But this device, planted on 28 June 1991, came with no warning and had been intended to kill a lot of people. It had been left outside the stage door of the Beck Theatre in Hayes in west London during an evening concert attended by up to 600 people and given by the band of the Blues and Royals cavalry regiment. The IRA had previous form when it came to attacking military musicians. In September the previous year, it had bombed the Royal Marines School of Music in Deal in Kent, killing eleven Marines and wounding twenty-one others.

Aware that the Blues and Royals could be a target, the theatre – a red-brick structure with interlocking grey-tiled roof elevations built in 1977 – and its parkland environs had been swept by police search teams before the concert. But it is likely the bomber was watching because he planted the device after the concert had started, when the coast was clear. It was delivered in a holdall, inside which a large lump of Semtex and a small rectangular plywood box containing the initiating mechanism – known in the trade as the time and power unit, or TPU – were concealed in a brown bag.

The concert went ahead without incident while a small circular memo-park timer inside the TPU steadily ticked down from a maximum delay position of 60 minutes. Unbeknown to the audience, or the musicians playing before them, the timer reached 'zero-hour', when the Semtex was supposed to tear through the building, but nothing happened. A tragedy had been averted, but the second act in this drama was about to begin.

After the concert had finished, the holdall was spotted by a member of the public, who alerted the police. Immediately realising this could be a bomb of some sort, the officers at the scene called in a colleague from the Met's own specialist bomb disposal unit, an Explosives Officer, known in the trade as an 'EXPO'.

Having originally trained with the army, the EXPO was almost certainly highly experienced in dealing with IRA devices, something that worked both to his advantage and against him on a day when he showed remarkable self-belief and confidence. After carefully approaching the holdall and satisfying himself that there was no booby trap, he opened it up and then slowly opened the brown bag inside. At that point he could see the TPU, the Semtex and two wires linking the TPU to the detonator that was protruding from the lump of explosive.

What he also saw was a lit torch bulb in one corner of the TPU where the top of the box was cut away. He would have recognised this from previous encounters with IRA TPUs. When the light was on it meant that the timer had expired, the circuit to the detonator was connected and the bomb was armed. Although he could not open the

TPU, the top of which was taped down, with the whole box almost certainly taped to the Semtex, he had a pretty good idea what the other components inside it would be. There would be a battery pack, the timer and a micro-switch, which served as a secondary safety device, allowing the bomber to deploy his bomb without fear of blowing himself up.

He would perhaps then have spent some minutes thinking through what he was seeing. The bomb should have gone off but it had not. He knew that because the light was on. The light also reminded him that the batteries were delivering power as intended. He reasoned that the micro-switch, meanwhile, must be in the 'on' position. He could see that a wooden dowel, which had been inserted through a hole in the box alongside the switch to depress its spring-loaded actuating button, had been removed. That meant the button was extended. It would be protruding from the side of the switch, meaning that, inside the switch, two metal contacts had closed together, connecting the circuit.

Often used to activate fridge lights when the door opens, micro-switches were, and are, widely available consumer electronics products. There was no particular record of them having failed in any way and not much reason to think this one could have malfunctioned.

Mulling it over, the EXPO almost certainly came to the conclusion that the fault in this case was either in the wiring or in the detonator. Of the two, the wiring was the most likely candidate, because commercially-produced detonators, such as the slender aluminium-encased one he was looking at, rarely failed. In contrast, the wiring was the bomb-maker's own work and had a more Heath Robinson feel, involving eight connection points, all of them buried in blobs of glue.

After considering his options – one of which was to deal with the device remotely, perhaps using a robot – the EXPO saw that he had a great opportunity to disarm the bomb and preserve it in its entirety as evidence. Successfully carrying out what the EXPOs called a 'manual render safe' would have been a huge coup against the IRA and a massive boost for the Met's hard-pressed anti-terrorist squad in their hunt for mainland 'sleeper' cells.

Driven on by the apparent certainty of his understanding of what he was looking at, the EXPO then reached into the brown bag inside the holdall and gently pulled the detonator out of the explosive. Step one. Then he picked up his cutters and reached in again to sever the red and black wires to the detonator. Step two. He had done it. The bomb was now safe and he must have thought his analysis had been spot on. This IRA bomb-maker had screwed up his wiring.

The following day I was sitting in the lab at the Fort with the TPU and the detonator from the Beck Theatre bomb in front of me. I had taken the Semtex to the explosives store after cutting the tape fixing the TPU to it. Later I would remove not just the remaining black electrical tape holding the explosive together but any remaining wrappers still coating the Semtex for fingerprint analysis.

Back in the lab I spent a few seconds considering what I was looking at. This was my first chance to examine the brains and control mechanism for an IRA bomb in pristine form. I was fixated by it and it felt like a big step for me. Normally, of course, we would have to make do with scavenging through the debris of a post-explosive scene to find tiny fragments of the components of a TPU – a slither of wire, a small chunk of battery, a crumb of glue or perhaps one numeral from the circular face of a car-parking timer. So this was pretty exciting, to put it mildly.

But why had it failed to detonate? Was the EXPO right to have come to the conclusion that it was either a faulty detonator or, much more likely, a failure in the wiring? At that point I had little reason to think he had been anything other than on the money. Just as he had observed, I could see the small bulb in the cutaway lower righthand corner of the box's lid – the sort you might find in a pocket torch or for use in a car interior. It was time to see the rest of it.

With my hands safely wrapped up in cotton gloves and then neoprene ones on top to safeguard against contaminating any fingerprint evidence, I used a scalpel to cut the black electrical tape that held the top of the box to the main body. Lifting it back, I could see the TPU just as the bomb-maker had created it. There were the power pack with four AA batteries held in a carrier, the memo-park timer and the micro-switch. Each component was anchored in blobs of thermoplastic adhesive – Hot Melt glue being the most likely proprietary brand – and linked by red and black wiring that led ultimately to the detonator.

This was classic IRA gear – a TPU arrangement that the organisation's quartermasters churned out in large numbers to supply their bombing campaigns in Ulster and on the British mainland. This was the mechanism that both ensured that a bomb exploded but also that it did not detonate while the bomber was deploying it. It was simple but effective.

The circuit ran from the batteries to a nail glued to the top of the timer that protruded horizontally from the circular revolving clock face. When the timer expired, this nail came into contact with a small metal post sticking up vertically in the centre of the box that was connected to both the light and the detonator. When the nail touched the post, the light came on and the detonator exploded, sending its shock wave through the Semtex. That would all happen, of course, as long as the dowel had been removed from the micro-switch.

I ran my eyes over the TPU for a few moments just to make sure I wasn't missing anything. Then I lowered my head to bench level so I could see from that angle that everything was as it should be. There was no obvious hardware failure – all the wiring connections looked solid enough. But I needed to check. So I picked up my voltage tester and gently applied its two prongs to each section of wire. It was all connected properly. What else could there be?

Perhaps the nail glued to the top of the timer had not connected properly to the small metal upright post in the centre of the main compartment when the timing period expired? But the two metal elements were snuggled up against each other just as they should be. I then examined the detonator, the two wires to which had been cut. Again I could see no evidence to suggest that this would not have worked once the timing mechanism had done its job.

That left the micro-switch.

At first glance I had assumed that the actuating button was fully extended in the 'out' or 'on' position, as you would expect once the dowel had been removed. (The dowel, incidentally, had been found inside the bag with the bomb, presumably left in there by the bomber on the basis that it would have been incinerated in the explosion, thus removing any fingerprint evidence on it). I had no real expectation of finding a fault in any aspect of the switch, but the more I looked at the actuating button, the more curious I became about its position. Was it fully extended or not? It was at that point that I lightly touched the end of the button with the prong from my voltmeter and felt it pop out.

'Hmmm, that's interesting,' I thought, 'so it's a bit sticky, a bit dodgy.' Then I tried to make it stay back where I had found it, but I couldn't do it. It remained fully extended as it should have been. 'Oh Christ, so it wasn't out – it had stayed in just once . . .'

Using a magnifying glass, I looked for a cause – something to explain why this tiny arm had failed to fully deploy and what was stopping it from releasing the circuit connectors inside the switch. I could see nothing. It was a freak failure and it was on that inexplicable occurrence that the EXPO's life had depended.

I worked hard to preserve as much fingerprint evidence as we could find from that bomb. The black tape that had held the box together and had been used to fix it to the Semtex was a good source of prints. Each section was carefully cut and pinned into a foam-lined box and sent to the police for analysis. I did the same with the remaining wrappers on the Semtex and the brown bag in which the bomb had been placed. It would prove very useful in linking the bomb-maker to the Beck Theatre attack.

It was ten months later that James Canning was arrested, an individual who would be described by the judge at his trial at the Old Bailey as an 'IRA quartermaster'. Aged thirty-five and Scottish-born, but raised in Northern Ireland, Canning had been living in London apparently as an ordinary citizen while secretly helping to plan and carry out attacks all over the capital. As cover he had met and moved in with Ethel Lamb, a lonely sixty-year-old local woman, with whom he had apparently fallen in love. He then used her home in Northholt in northwest London as a base for his bomb-making operations in late 1991 and early 1992.

However, the police were watching him, and on his arrest in April 1992 they matched his fingerprints to the brown bag in which the Beck Theatre bomb had been planted. At Lamb's home, and in a nearby lock-up garage, police found more than 84lb of Semtex – enough for scores of bombs – and timers and power units, including one with an anti-handling device designed to injure bomb disposal officers. They also found incendiary devices and six Kalashnikov rifles, including one that had been used in an assassination attempt on Sir Peter Terry, the former governor of Gibraltar. The one thing missing – and which was evidently holding Canning back – was a stock of detonators.

Canning was linked not only to the Beck Theatre bomb but a series of firebomb attacks on shops in central London and a similar attack on the National Gallery. He was also alleged to have been heavily involved in the attacks on mainline stations plus a series of smaller devices in the Whitehall area, including a briefcase bomb that exploded without injury and a device in a telephone kiosk that was defused.

EXPLOSIVE

I knew perhaps better than anybody – apart, that is, from the EXPO in this case – exactly what Mr Justice Leonard meant when he told Canning that only 'extraordinary good fortune' had prevented a major atrocity at Beck Theatre. Canning was sentenced to thirty years in jail after being found guilty of conspiring to cause explosions and possessing enough Semtex to build eighty bombs. He was released in the wake of the Good Friday Agreement in 1998.

I never forgot the Beck Theatre case and used it often in my training talks, especially with young bomb disposal officers. It was the perfect illustration of why it is always necessary to keep an open mind when dealing with improvised explosives and question and deconstruct every conclusion you reach. More than anything it underlined the potentially fatal consequences of making assumptions without the visual evidence to back them up. If in doubt, I would urge them, take the safe route, which, in this case, would have meant using a robot.

8

Lorry bombs on the mainland: a deadly game of cat and mouse with the IRA

I had a bit of fun with the Stoke Newington lorry bomb in November 1992. When everybody had finished with the truck – by that I mean forensic scientists from the FEL and our counterparts in the Metropolitan Police, including fingerprint experts, tool mark experts and fibres experts – I needed to weigh it.

That meant I had to be able to drive the 10-tonne Volvo box lorry, in which the Provisional IRA had cleverly concealed a massive bomb, on to the weighbridge at the Fort. But the scavenging of forensic samples to build a case for use in the trial of an IRA suspect then in custody in connection with the discovery of the device meant that most of the wiring from the dashboard had been disconnected or cut and both the doors had been removed.

It was like being back in my teenage years, mucking about with cars and bikes. I had a quick look where the glove box had been removed and worked out how to 'hot-wire' a vehicle that the IRA had intended to use against the

117

City of London. They had intended this device to follow the huge blasts seven months earlier, in April 1992, from bombs concealed in a lorry at the Baltic Exchange, and in a van at Staples Corner, a major road junction in north London.

I am sure some of my colleagues raised the odd eyebrow when they saw me driving that blue doorless truck around the FEL site, especially since it was still full of explosive. The object was to get it on the weighbridge, then take it back to the bay where we were working on it, remove all the explosive, and then weigh it again. That way I would be able to calculate the size of the bomb discovered in Stoke Newington, and it was a whopper – the biggest single device we had ever dealt with at the Fort at that time, clocking in at 3.2 tonnes.

The explosive concealed in the back was a mix of ammonium nitrate – otherwise known as fertiliser and available in garden centres and farm suppliers – and sugar. Icing sugar, in fact, which mixes down far better than caster sugar or granulated sugar. These ingredients would have been combined using a cement mixer at a makeshift secret bomb factory, almost certainly in Northern Ireland.

The total weight of the mix was equivalent to about 100 large bags of fertiliser combined with 150 of the sort of bags of icing sugar that you might buy in the supermarket. Had this detonated, it would have caused massive damage to any urban area, much as the two bombs at, respectively, Staples Corner and the Baltic Exchange had done.

Lorry bombs on the mainland

The Baltic Exchange device had detonated on the evening of 10 April 1992, after the IRA drove a large white truck into the City and abandoned it on St Mary Axe. The bomb was estimated to be only one-third of the size of the one discovered at Stoke Newington, but it was still the biggest device to explode on mainland Britain since the Second World War and it wrecked the Baltic Exchange, killing three people and injuring ninety-one others.

The advent of lorry bombs in the early 1990s marked a new tactic in the IRA mainland campaign, as the republican terrorist group dramatically increased the scale of destruction it was able to inflict on British cities. Some of these devices were constructed in Britain itself and then deployed, while others were shipped across the Irish Sea on ferries and then driven to their targets by IRA terrorists operating on the mainland.

Of course the big problem the IRA had was how to conceal these bombs. They couldn't just heap up a load of explosive in the back of a lorry, stick a detonator in it and expect it not to be seen by police or anyone else who happened to peer in for whatever reason. The reality was they were playing a deadly cat and mouse game with the police and they had to come up with ever more ingenious ways of concealing bombs to give themselves a chance of getting the lorries to their targets without detection.

The Stoke Newington device was seized purely by chance and only because the driver and his accomplice lost their nerve. They were stopped by police on the A10 in north London in the early hours of the morning because the lorry had a faulty tail light. Assuming the police had been tipped off, the two men jumped down from the cab and ran. One of them, Patrick Kelly, was later arrested after a police hunt. The other escaped after shooting a policeman who was chasing him. Fortunately the officer survived, while Kelly, aged forty, was eventually sentenced to twenty-five years in jail.

Initially the lorry was examined at the scene on Stoke Newington Road by police officers, who had quickly realised something must be up. The behaviour of the two men apart, what gave the game away was a white coloured wire, which they recognised as detonating cord. This was concealed in a length of black ribbed plastic hose that had been fitted between the cab and the freight compartment of the lorry. At the cab end, the cord – which I later confirmed contained PETN high explosive – was sticking out of the hose and had two reels of adhesive tape hanging from it, ready to attach it to detonators.

Elsewhere in the cab there were two standard IRA time and power units (TPUs) – more or less identical to the ones found with the IRA Beck Theatre bomb – featuring memo-park timers and with small aluminium-bodied detonators attached. (The second TPU and detonator had been deployed purely as a fail-safe in case the first timer had ticked down and, for some reason, not worked.)

By that point the officers had no doubt there must be a bomb in the back of the lorry and they called in an EXPO, who set about trying to work out what the detonating cord was attached to.

Aware that they could be booby-trapped, the EXPO began by carefully prising open the rear doors of the freight compartment and was confronted with a stack of plasterboard. At the side door to the compartment he found something similar, the side-ends or off-cuts of seventy-six plasterboard sheets.

He knew the bomb had to be in that compartment somewhere. As he slowly slid the top plasterboard sheet away, he uncovered a secret compartment created in a space where all the plasterboard, apart from the top sheet, had been cut out. The compartment was covered and lined in black plastic and, inside it, the beige-coloured explosive was packed behind a makeshift wooden partition, complete with bracing supports. This was a quite impressive concealment of a very powerful device that would have aroused no suspicion had an officer simply stopped the vehicle and asked to have a look in the back.

The EXPO then started digging into the mixture using a small trowel and brushes, intent on removing three booster devices that had been implanted in it. These were long steel poles – not unlike scaffolding poles – into which the ammonium and sugar mix had been densely packed and through which ran detonator cord. The purpose of the boosters was to create intense explosive reactions along their length, which would ensure that the entire mix went up when the signal came through from the TPU.

Why were the IRA concerned that this explosive reaction might not happen? Well, early in the Troubles the advent of bombs using fertiliser in Northern Ireland prompted the authorities to issue new rules governing the maximum amount of nitrate – nitrogen being the key explosive ingredient – allowed in commercially-produced fertiliser. It was restricted from 35% in pure ammonium nitrate to a maximum of 26%, and an inert mineral called dolomite was added to the mix instead. This meant that the IRA could no longer rely on a simple fertiliser and sugar mix detonating satisfactorily – it would need help.

After some minutes digging into the hard-packed material, the EXPO decided that trying to remove the booster poles in the middle of a built-up area was not the most sensible course of action. A decision was taken to tow the lorry, using a goods vehicle recovery truck, to the Fort, the least risky of the options open to the police. So, later that same morning, I was on hand to receive the lorry and its cargo when it arrived at the FEL.

Over the next couple of days I helped supervise the various forensics teams looking for evidence to link Kelly with the bomb. Once that work was finished, I dug out the booster tubes and emptied them, which took some time. Then I conducted a series of tests to determine what the bomb-makers had used in the mixture. Identifying the sugar was interesting because while chemical analysis of the white powder in the mix showed it to be predominantly sucrose, it also contained around 1.2% calcium phosphate. That is one of a few types of anti-caking agents used in the sugar industry that is added in small quantities to icing sugar (which is sucrose) to prevent it from caking in storage.

I also conducted a simple test to demonstrate that this 'improvised mixture' would explode if detonated adequately and that it could correctly be deemed high explosive. Defence barristers did not have to explain why the materials had been found in the arrangement discovered in the lorry and I knew they would try to argue that the mixture was not capable of exploding and thus could not be a bomb. The so-called Gap test involved detonating a sample of inert material – say sand, for example – in a small tube and comparing the damage to the tube when a sample of the mix from the lorry was introduced in its place. The results were dramatic, with the tube distorted and torn in the first case but stripped into small separate fragments in the second example.

Once we had taken samples of the explosive for our own use in evidence, the mix was broken down using water jets, which cut into it and washed it out of the lorry into a paddling pool-type inflatable container. From there it was hoovered up by a sewerage clean-up lorry with a powerful vacuum hose – known as a sludge gulper – and taken away to be disposed of. I am not sure what happened to it – it may even have been taken to a farm for spreading on the land. The lorry itself was almost certainly scrapped.

Four months before the discovery of this device, police in London had seized an articulated lorry with a number of partially-constructed IRA lorry bombs in it and a Ford van that had a device all wired up and ready to go. From those finds we knew the IRA were using an ammonium nitrate and sugar mix on the mainland and that they were likely to be using booster tubes, but I have to say I was still impressed by what they had done with the Stoke Newington device, and the elaborate way it was concealed and put together with booster tubes.

In my evidence at the trial of Patrick Kelly, I concluded: 'This was a viable improvised explosive device, which, if it had functioned, would have caused enormous damage to property within at least 200 metres. It had the capacity to destroy brick, concrete or metal-braced structures in its immediate vicinity, and to kill or cause serious injury to people in the surrounding area, either from direct blast, collapsing buildings or flying debris.'

The cat-and-mouse game continued with the IRA getting through with a massive lorry bomb that wrecked Bishopsgate in London in April 1993. That blast killed one person and injured forty-four others and caused damage worth more than £350 million, including destroying St Ethelburga's church and wrecking Liverpool Street station. The attack resulted in the police imposing a 'ring of steel' set of security measures to protect the City from further bombings.

But the IRA kept changing their tactics and their methods of disguising bombs on lorries and, eighteen months after the Stoke Newington bomb was discovered, we saw perhaps the high point of their ingenuity when a white Leyland lorry turned up at Heysham Docks near Lancaster. This looked, to all the world, like an empty flatbed truck with no cargo on it and no box structure on the back to hide anything in either.

But this was another three-tonne bomb that could have inflicted devastation. Detectives believed it could have been intended for the City of London or for another strategic target, such as the Channel Tunnel. The lorry had arrived on a ferry from Warren Point in Northern Ireland and had been seized after an intelligence tip-off. No one turned up at the docks to collect it.

In this case the same ammonium nitrate and sugar mix had been used, but instead of concealing it inside a consignment of builders' materials, the bomb-makers had filled the flatbed itself – a 25 ft-long rectangular void about 8–10 ft in depth. Once again they had used booster tubes running the length of the lorry, and in the central area of the flatbed they had enlarged the depth slightly to accommodate more mixture and two more boosters. The only external modification that was detectable was a couple of small holes that had been drilled in the end of the flatbed and which had been used to slide the booster tubes in. But even these had been concealed with back-plugs welded in.

The connection via detonating cord to the cab was carried out far more subtly than at Stoke Newington, with the cord running hidden between the flatbed and the cab and emerging into the cab into a fixed toolbox underneath the dashboard, where the TPUs were hidden from view. You could walk around that lorry and see nothing – no cargo, no space for a bomb and no wiring linking anything to the cab. A cursory inspection of the cab, meanwhile, would reveal nothing unless you happened to look in the tool box.

This one wasn't my case, but, like most of my colleagues, I was intrigued to see the Leyland when it arrived at the FEL, where the whole thing was weighed and dismantled just as we had done with the Stoke Newington device. Again I had no doubt that this one was a viable device – the depth of mix was narrow because of the confines of the flatbed base, but the inclusion of four booster tubes running the length of the freight platform would have ensured that this device would have gone up.

After Heysham, the lorry bombs kept coming, with the last ones getting through at Canary Wharf in London in

Lorry bombs on the mainland

February 1996, which killed two people and devastated a wide area, and finally in Manchester city centre, in June that year, which injured 212 people and caused damage worth £700 million. Looking back, my view of the IRA has not changed since those days – I considered what they were doing was cowardly, unnecessary and evil. But my grudging respect for their ingenuity in disguising their handiwork remains undimmed.

9

The IRA try to light the gas

Late on the night of 25 February 1993, Denis Kinsella, a 25-year-old unemployed roofer from Nottingham, drove his battered Mazda van towards Longford gas storage facility, owned by British Gas, at Winwick Road in Warrington in Cheshire.

This was an extensive site with three large gas holders or gasometers, vast circular structures that were used to store thousands of cubic metres of gas.

Next to them, in a separate section, gas was being stored at high pressure in ten cylindrically-shaped 50-metre-long tanks. These were stacked on top of each other in two layers of five. The high-pressure tanks ran hard up against a dual carriageway, on the other side of which was an extensive area of housing.

Alongside Kinsella in the van that night were Pairic MacFhloinn, aged forty, who had a long background in republican extremism, and a third man, Michael Timmins, eighteen, who was alleged to have helped build the bombs they deployed but who would never be apprehended.

The IRA try to light the gas

While Kinsella waited near the site, the other two men managed to gain access to the facility and then planted three bombs and three incendiary devices. They positioned two bombs and incendiaries on two of the gasometers and a third bomb, with an incendiary, underneath one of the high-pressure cylinders.

With their work done, the IRA gang got back in the van just before midnight and Kinsella set off to make their getaway. But within minutes they were spotted by Constable Mark Toker, while the van was waiting at a red light, and he approached the van on foot and began to question them.

When PC Toker told them he wanted to search the van, MacFhloinn drew a 9mm automatic pistol and fired five shots, hitting the policeman three times at point-blank range. As the van sped off, a nurse who happened to be passing by rushed to PC Toker's aid – he would go on to be very lucky indeed and survive the attack – and the alarm was raised.

The gang subsequently hijacked a car, locking its owner in the boot. But following a high-speed chase with police, during which shots were fired, the car was stopped on the motorway not far from Warrington, and MacFhloinn and Kinsella were arrested while Timmins made good his escape.

At just after 4 a.m., about 3½ hours after the arrests, the bombs at the gasworks went off, the most visible and audible evidence of which was a huge fireball that filled the night sky as one of the gasometers ignited. What had transpired with the other two bombs was not immediately clear.

I was given this case, but to start with I went nowhere near Warrington. British Gas spent several days making the site safe and removing all the remaining gas stored there, which took some time. There were other things to deal with as well, not least an arms cache found in Kinsella's allotment that included a quantity of Semtex plastic explosive.

Just over three weeks after the gasworks bombing, the IRA retaliated for the arrests of MacFhloinn and Kinsella by planting two bombs in litter bins in Bridge Street in Warrington. They detonated a hundred yards apart outside branches of Boots and McDonald's, and within a minute of each other at lunchtime. The result was carnage, with two children killed and fifty-six people injured.

I finally got up to Warrington just after those bombings, which claimed the lives of three-year-old Johnathan Ball and twelve-year-old Tim Parry. The atmosphere in the town was still one of grief and shock at the sheer brutality of what the IRA had done. The cell that planted the litter bin bombs had made a warning call, but the police said it was misleading and did not mention Warrington, giving them no time to clear the area. I met some of the police officers who had collected samples of the shrapnel and fragments of the control units for the bombs that I had looked through in the lab at the Fort. No one would ever be brought to trial for that outrage.

After visiting the scene in Bridge Street, it was time to have a look at the gasworks. I knew that incendiary devices had been used in the attack, the first of its kind on mainland Britain, but I was not sure how or why they had been deployed. It was not long into my tour of the facility, however, that it became clear to me that this had been a carefully pre-planned and thought-out operation that could have had catastrophic consequences.

While one gasometer was destroyed, the other was just dented and not breached. Significantly, the remains of an incendiary device had been found just far enough away from the direct blast field for it not to have been destroyed by the explosion, leaving it to burn freely on its own.

Moving to the cylindrical high-pressure storage section, I found a similar pattern. A bomb that I later estimated to consist of around 2–4kg of Semtex, with a timing device, had been placed underneath one of the tubes – which alone contained around 14,000 cubic metres of gas – and the charred remains of an incendiary had been found just far enough away not to have been damaged by the initial explosion. The detonation under the cylinder had caused serious damage to the steel structure on which the tube sat in a layer of cladding, but it had not breached the tube itself.

'Jesus, that was a piece of luck,' I muttered to myself, as I surveyed the blast site, listening to a police officer informing me quite confidently – and incorrectly – that if the cylinder had been breached the whole thing would have 'taken off like a rocket'.

I was more interested in why the bomb had not pierced the cylinder. It looked to me as though the bombers had not been able to find a way to attach their device to the underside of the curved belly of the tube. Unable to climb on top of the tank, they had had to place it on the ground underneath, in the hope that it would still have enough reach and explosive force to breach the cylinder.

But the pattern was clear: these guys knew something about gas explosions. They had used their bombs to try to breach the gasometers and the high-pressure cylinder and then deployed the incendiaries – also on timers and con- sisting of slow-burning gunpowder – to ignite the resulting mix of air and gas. The bombers knew that gas on its own would not ignite, but when mixed with oxygen and set alight, it could burn in the form of a fireball or explode.

In the case of the gasometer that had not gone up, it was purely a stroke of luck that the device had not managed to pierce the outer skin, leaving the structure intact. It took some time to work out what had happened to the gasometer that now lay in ruins. It was clear from the wreckage that the bomb had been placed on the walkway around the base of the uppermost section and was thus quite close to the roof. When it detonated, it blasted a hole in the side of the gasometer, but shrapnel almost certainly pierced the roof. In this instance the incendiary seemed to have been placed too far away from the seat of the explosion and I judged that it had played no role in what happened next.

The methane gas contained in this large circular tank – which was stored at just above atmospheric pressure, just sufficient to lift the gasometer sections – then began escaping through the holes in the roof. These would have been hot because of the explosive action of shrapnel that created them. As the gas escaped and then mixed with the surrounding air, it would thus have caught fire. This would have gradually heated the remains of the roof, which then peeled back as more and more gas started to burn.

Ultimately this process tore the roof off completely and allowed a cloud of gas to develop that burned at its edges and gradually towards the centre, eventually creating the impression of a fireball that towered high into the Warrington night sky and terrified those who saw it from close by. Although this was a devastating outcome, it could have been far worse if the gas had been under greater pressure, something that would have created more turbulence and more efficient mixing with oxygen as it escaped. In that scenario a far more explosive mixture would have resulted . . . which brings me back to the high-pressure cylinders.

Over several weeks of careful thought, during which period I discussed this with people at British Gas on an informal basis and officials at the Forensic Science Service, who specialize in fire and explosions, I worked out what I thought the bombers were trying to achieve. One scenario posited the idea that the explosion tore an eight-inch hole in the cylinder under which the bomb was placed. This was the largest hole that British Gas believed a tank could sustain without suffering a total collapse.

In this instance the gas, which was being stored at a pressure of 100–350psi, would have started escaping very fast. So fast, in fact, that it would be very unlikely to ignite from the heat of the explosion. And because it was being released from high pressure, it would also be very cold and would be creating a high degree of turbulence as it mixed with the surrounding air. The net result would be an ever-expanding relatively dense and cool cloud of mixed gas and air.

In this setting the incendiary – its activation delayed slightly to allow the gas and air mix to form – was potentially devastating. Once ignited the cloud could explode, as I put it in a subsequent internal briefing paper, 'in the generally accepted, ringing in the ears, houses falling down, trousers turning brown, sense of the word'. In my judgement, such an explosion would have caused the failure of one or more of the adjacent tanks and the people living in the homes just a few hundred yards away from the tanks on the other side of the dual carriageway would have been in mortal danger in such an eventuality.

The IRA try to light the gas

A second scenario put them and many others in far greater peril. This posited an explosion causing a sufficiently large hole in the cylinder immediately above the bomb to cause it to catastrophically fail and rupture. British Gas advised that should that happen the forces released would then lead to the failure of the adjacent tanks, which would then all collapse in an almighty physical explosion that would release not 100 tonnes of gas, as in scenario one, but 1,000 tonnes. This huge cloud, which would be mixing violently with air, would be ignited either by the destructive forces released in the break-up of the tanks or by the incendiary. That ignition might have caused an actual gas explosion, or a very large and vigorously burning gas cloud. Either way the result would have been damage on a massive scale, leading to very significant loss of life in the houses adjacent to the facility.

The more I mulled this over, the more convinced I became that MacFhloinn and Timmins knew exactly what they were up to. This wasn't going to be just another infrastructure target that would cost a few million pounds to rebuild. This was a no-warning attack that aimed to cause possibly the greatest loss of life of any IRA bombing on mainland Britain. The trouble was that, as their trial grew ever closer, the prosecution could find no one to explain this apart from me.

I knew my limits and knew where my expertise lay. It was in the make-up of improvised bombs and the behaviour

135

of explosives, not the behaviour of gas clouds, a highly technical specialist subject on which this case would turn. Initially I hoped that someone from British Gas would step in. But in my discussions with their technical staff it became increasingly clear that this was not going to happen. I surmised that they were terrified of ending up in the dock themselves, as it were, for having built such a massive gas storage facility in a location where so many people's lives could be put at risk by it. They were also very reluctant to go on the record admitting just how big a disaster this could have been.

Another option was the experts at the Forensic Science Service, but they were reluctant too. The problem for them was that this involved bombs, which was not their area of expertise. And the sheer scale of what could have happened was completely outside their compass – they were used to dealing with small fires and explosions, not vast rolling fireballs crossing roads and engulfing houses and everyone in them.

I remember the sinking feeling during my discussions with them when I made the mistake of mentioning that, during the ten years before I joined the FEL, I had worked at the Health & Safety Executive (HSE). While there I had spent some time working with inspectors in assessing the hazards of materials released from pressurised containers, including natural gas, using the HSE's own computer models. On hearing this, they reacted as if they were off the hook and I was very much on it. 'You'll be fine, Cliff, go for it,' I was told. 'Otherwise those guys are going to get away with it.'

It occurred to me that perhaps the HSE itself might put someone up. But, just like the others, they did not want to get involved and they did not want their computer models used in open court. We could have gone through a long and arduous legal process to access them, but it was not going to be a satisfactory way of dealing with the expert-witness element.

It was almost exactly a year after the attack that the trial took place at the Old Bailey. In the build-up I spent many a sleepless night worrying about the task I was taking on. Most people in the lab would have had no qualms about just firmly saying 'No, this is not my area.' But I knew I had some experience with my work at the HSE. The question was – and I must have asked myself this a hundred times over – was it enough to make me an expert?

There is one golden rule as far as court appearances go in the expert-witness field and that is never stray outside your area of competence, whatever the temptation to do so. I was about to come as close as I ever would to breaking that rule. There is no doubt that I was keen to see the perpetrators of this attack get an appropriate sentence for what they had really intended, not what had happened. But there was a deeper feeling of responsibility too – that sense that the IRA could not be allowed to get away with it and

I could not shirk this, whatever the risks to my professional reputation.

As the trial progressed I knew exactly what was coming. After I had given my evidence for the prosecution, explaining what I thought MacFhloinn et al had been planning, their defence teams would try to destroy my credibility. And sure enough, when Rock Tansey, QC, got to his feet, he went on the attack just as I expected.

I can still remember the flesh-crawling sensation on the back of my neck as he set about demonstrating to the jury that I was hopelessly out of my depth. The exchanges went something like this:

'Right, Mr Todd, you are an expert on gas clouds, gas explosions and the modelling of them are you?'

'Well, I consider I have a sufficient grounding in the subject to offer an informed opinion to the court.'

'An informed opinion, eh?'

'Yes.'

'Well, let's find out just exactly *how* informed you are, Mr Todd.'

I swallowed hard – this was like being ritually humiliated in front of the whole school. But I needed to stay calm at all costs.

'Have you read this?' Tansey held up a suitably technical work on the chemistry of gas clouds and their behaviour, enunciating its title clearly for the jury to hear.

'No, I have not.'

'And what about this?' Another text was brandished before the court.

'No, not that one either.'

'And this?' A third volume enjoyed its moment in the spotlight.

'No, I don't believe I have –'

'And finally this, Mr Todd,' he cried, with a flourish, expecting a full house, as it were, of unread texts.

But I had read *The Investigation & Control of Gas Explosions in Buildings and Heating Plant*, by a certain R. J. Harris, and I was able to puncture his balloon for a second by informing him as such.

But Rock Tansey was not going to be derailed that easily.

'So you have read just one of the four, Mr Todd? That's not sufficient to make you an expert, is it?'

'Well . . .'

'I put it to you that you clearly have next to no experience in this area and you are not qualified to help this court on the subject of gas explosions.'

At that point I explained to him about the work I had done with the HSE.

'Oh, the Health & Safety Executive? Exactly what sites did you look at for them, Mr Todd? And what conclusions did you reach on their behalf?'

At this point things became even more tense because I told him I did not want to disclose work done for a previous employer, much of which, I explained, was in any case irrelevant to this case.

It was time to bail me out. John Nutting, counsel for the prosecution, rose to request that the jury be cleared from the court so that legal discussion over my fitness to give evidence might take place. I then sat impassively listening to my career as an expert witness being fought over, as Mr Justice McCullough balanced Tansey on the one hand with Nutting on the other.

Eventually the judge came to a decision. He said that, on the subject of gas clouds, he was satisfied that I knew enough to assist the court. 'But it is open to you, Mr Tansey,' he said, 'to persuade the jury that he doesn't know much about it. If you say that Mr Todd is not a proper expert, that his opinion does not carry much weight, I will leave it to the jury to make up their own minds on his fitness or otherwise.'

It was hardly a ringing endorsement, but I could finally breathe a big sigh of relief – the pressure was off. I had convinced the judge that I knew enough. Tansey was not finished, however. I spent three days altogether giving evidence and being cross-examined by him, and by Michael Mansfield and Helena Kennedy for the other defendants.

Tansey got particularly exercised by something he read in a text entitled 'Understanding vapour cloud explosions – an experimental study', another work by R. J. Harris. He read out a summary by Harris explaining that 'vapour cloud explosions . . . cannot be produced by combustion of a cloud which is literally unconfined'. If this was the case, Tansey was arguing, then the IRA bombers could not have anticipated that the gas escaping from high-pressure tanks at Warrington could have exploded.

I pointed out to him that he had conveniently missed out the middle of the sentence. In full, it read: 'Vapour cloud explosions can be produced by combustion within a region of close-packed obstacles formed by process pipe-work and vessels, but cannot be produced by combustion of a cloud which is literally unconfined.'

This was then followed by a vigorous disagreement between us over whether the site at Warrington contained obstacles or not. I was clear – for the purposes of the defin-itions used in the passage quoted – that the Warrington site was most definitely a 'region' of close-packed obstacles, with other tanks, pipework and houses all in the vicinity.

I stuck to my guns throughout about the possibility of grave consequences for the residents of the housing estate. But I was careful not to be too specific about the sheer size and scope of a huge explosion that could have taken place, confining myself to the phrase 'a very violent event'. The judge seemed to understand my reluctance to go into specifics. 'Yes, I expect you would need to be in the Nevada desert to test something like that, wouldn't you?' he said. 'Yes, your honour, that's right,' I replied.

EXPLOSIVE

At the end of my three days in the witness box, I was delighted to finally hear the judge utter the immortal words: 'Thank you, Mr Todd.' But I had one fright to come. Just as I stepped down into the well of the court, a member of the jury leant across towards me and mouthed the words 'Well done!' I could have run a mile. I was absolutely terrified at the thought that all that work we had done was about to be thrown out and a new trial ordered. I thrust my head away as if I had heard nothing and made for the exit at high speed.

After a five-week trial, MacFhloinn, Kinsella and John Kinsella, Denis Kinsella's uncle, were all convicted. Mac-Fhloinn was handed a thirty-five-year sentence for his role in the bombings, a tariff that reflected the full scale of what he had intended that night. Mr Justice McCullough told MacFhloinn that he was satisfied that the way they had positioned the bombs indicated that he intended to cause 'the maximum effect possible with the materials available' and risked the lives of those on the housing estate nearby. 'I am satisfied that danger to life was likely; to the firemen called to the scene, the users of the main road and to the lives of those asleep in their houses,' he said. 'Their lives and safety were at risk from fire, from the escape of gas which you intended. Had one or more of the high-pressure tanks exploded, the effects would have been far reaching in extent and severity both to persons and property.'

The IRA try to light the gas

I can't say I felt much more than a sense of grim satisfaction. I had strayed outside my comfort zone and had learned a lesson. I would not be stepping so close to the limits of my expertise again. Three days in the witness box, much of it given over to hostile questioning, was an ordeal not to be repeated.

10

Israeli embassy: something we had never seen before

You never knew what you were going to find in this job. The next bomb-maker might be a genius or an improviser or someone who was stuck for the right ingredients and made do with what he or she could find. The main thing, as a forensic explosives scientist, was to try to keep an open mind and keep asking yourself what the evidence was telling you.

The FEL's investigation into the Palestinian terrorist bombings of the Israeli embassy in London and a Jewish community centre in Finchley in the north of the city in the summer of 1994 demonstrated just how difficult it was to work out what ingredients were in a device when we had not seen them being used in that way before.

It was an episode that also underlined, just as the IRA Beck Theatre case had, how dangerous it was to make assumptions about what you were seeing. In this case, someone's wrong guesswork led to a situation where volatile high explosive was brought unprotected, as it were, into the FEL reception on the basis that it was relatively harmless. It could have killed everyone in the room . . .

It was shortly after midday on 26 July, a hot summer's day, when a smartly-dressed woman drove a grey Audi with false number plates through the police checkpoint at Kensington Palace Gardens in West London – one of the capital's most expensive addresses and home to several foreign missions – and parked it next to the Israeli embassy.

She got out of the car and told an armed diplomatic protection officer who challenged her that she was visiting friends in apartments next door to the embassy but had to go to Kensington High Street to buy some cigarettes. A few seconds after she disappeared from view, the car exploded. It was hurled 50ft into the air and a witness described seeing debris flying 100ft above the treetops. Thirteen people were injured – miraculously none seriously – in a blast that damaged the perimeter wall and front elevation of the embassy and an adjoining garage block. It also blew out windows in nearby shops and offices, as well as in Kensington Palace.

At that time we were extremely busy at the Fort and this case was the last thing we needed. We had been dealing with intense IRA activity on the mainland for years and resources were stretched to breaking point. Three senior case officers had left the service since 1989, leaving myself and only one other officer with proper operational experience. Below us there was only a handful of trainees, who were either not doing their own cases or were only taking on minor ones.

The caseload at that time included dozens of IRA devices in London, most of them small-scale attacks or incendiary devices in shops, designed to create fear and confusion. There had been an improvised mortar attack on Heathrow airport, a booby-trap bomb delivered to a chip shop in Yorkshire, six similar devices sent to the Stena Line ferry company and to several farming businesses, a well-disguised IRA lorry bomb intercepted at Heysham docks in Liverpool, an incendiary device at a factory in Cambridge and a car bomb in Croydon.

So, when we got the call to head to Kensington Palace Gardens, there was a feeling of 'not this, not now'.

I went in support of Lisa Brown, the most experienced case officer in our department, apart from our boss, Allen Feraday. We got to the scene several hours after the explosion and were impressed by the state of devastation. The car used by the bombers was completely wrecked. There was rubble all over the road where the perimeter wall of the embassy had been breached and both of us fairly quickly came to the conclusion that this was the work of a high explosive device probably weighing in the region of 20–30lb.

At that stage we assumed the bombers must have used a commercially-available high explosive – possibly a plastic explosive used by the military, like Semtex, or perhaps gelignite, used for blasting in the mining industry. This was an unusual attack in London at that time, with its origins and apparent motivations in Middle Eastern politics.

At first it was blamed by British security sources on Iranian-backed extremists linked to the Lebanon-based Hezbollah group, but responsibility for it was later claimed by the hitherto unknown 'Jaffa Unit' of the 'Palestinian Resistance'. The assumption was that it was carried out in protest at the settlement then being negotiated by the Palestinian leader, Yasser Arafat, with Israel. The bombing would go on to become the focus of continued controversy amid claims the British government had been warned of an attack in advance.

Either way, on that summer's afternoon in west London, we knew we were dealing with bomb-makers we had not encountered before.

We took some samples, swabbed some surfaces for analysis back at the Fort and agreed with the police what the priority items were for recovery to the FEL for further analysis. I felt sure we would be able to establish the basic ingredients of what had been a major explosive device that could have killed so many people in the heart of the capital.

Shortly after midnight that day, another car bomb exploded, this time in the north London suburb of Finchley, outside Balfour House. This is a Jewish community centre, about five miles from the embassy, which housed the London offices of, among others, the Jewish Agency for Israel, the Joint Israel Appeal and the World Zionist Organisation. The building had previously been strengthened against attack with protected windows and double doors, so much of the blast was reflected back into the street, where it smashed glass in a bus stop and nearby shop windows and injured six people. The bomb had been placed in a Triumph Acclaim car.

While Lisa continued to lead on the embassy bomb, this explosion was assigned to me. When I got the call in the early hours, I agreed with the police at the scene what to look for in terms of collecting evidence and did not attend in person.

In the weeks that followed, we duly tested all the samples we had from both scenes and we found almost nothing to suggest what the bomb-makers had used, apart from some fragments of PP3 batteries. We used screen tests for commercially-produced organic explosive compounds – in other words carbon-based explosives that would be our prime suspects – and nothing matched.

Every now and again, a bomb would detonate with such efficiency – and this happened occasionally with IRA devices – that no residue was left at the scene of any kind, or at least that could be detected in sufficient quantities to be regarded as significant. Hard-pressed as she was, and with a huge workload on her hands, Lisa was content to draw a line under the case and concluded that this was an

Policemen walk away from the cockpit of the 747 Pan Am airliner that exploded and crashed over Lockerbie, Scotland, 22 December 1988. All 243 passengers and 16 crew members were killed as well as 11 Lockerbie residents. In 2003, Libya admitted responsibility.

Remote-controlled robot checking vet Dr Max Headley's car after the Animal Liberation Front placed a bomb under it. Dr Headley luckily escaped serious injury, but John Cupper, a 13-month-old baby in a pushchair on the pavement was severely injured by shrapnel from the blast.

Rather chaotic treatment of the scene-of-crash for the Lauda Air aircraft in Thailand, 1991.

Above. Damage to the Baltic Exchange in St Mary Axe, London, by a one-ton IRA truck bomb in 1992. The building was eventually demolished and redeveloped into the Swiss Re building, now commonly known as the Gherkin.

Left. The floral memorial shrine to two young victims killed by an IRA bomb in the centre of Warrington, Cheshire, 27 February 1993. Two small bombs exploded in litter bins outside a Boots store and a McDonald's restaurant, killing two children and injuring many other people. Although warnings had been sent, the area was not evacuated in time.

Above. Aftermath of a car bomb outside the Israeli Embassy in London, 1994. This was followed a few hours later by another car bomb outside a Jewish community hub in Finchley. Jawad Botmeh and Samar Alami, both Palestinians, were later sentenced to 20 years for these bombings.

Below, right. Scene of devastation at London Docklands South Quay after the IRA detonated a powerful truck bomb on 9 February 1996, killing two and causing £150 million worth of damage.

Francisco de Sá Carneiro, Prime Minister of Portugal, was among seven people killed in 1980 when a twin-engined Cessna 421A light aircraft crashed shortly after take-off from Lisbon airport.

Above, left. Icelandic singer Björk at the 1998 Brit Awards, previously the intended recipient of an acid bomb from stalker Ricardo López in 1996. Fortunately, the package was intercepted before delivery.

Above, right. Jonathan Wilkes, a former magistrate, was convicted and sentenced to 5 years, later raised to 8 years, for making several sophisticated pipe bombs 'with intent to endanger life'. Fortunately they were found before he could deploy them, and the intended target or targets were never satisfactorily established.

Below. Stephen Menary, victim of the torch bomb at the White City TA base in 2001. Here, pictured later with other members of his Army Cadet group.

Above. Getting into character during a major incident exercise with police and first responders.

Below. Test firing a rocket-propelled grenade in Bulgaria, 2001.

Above. Fiery aftermath of the truck bomb outside Sari Club, Kuta, Bali, 2002.

Below, left. Saajit Badat, shoe bomber copycat, 2004.

Below, right. Dhiren Barot, architect of the 'Gas Limos Project' in 2004, for which he was convicted and received a 40-year sentence, subsequently reduced to 30 years by the Court of Appeal.

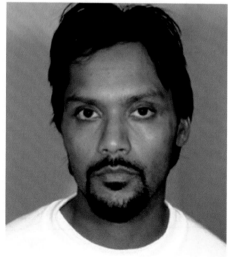

Damage to an underground train at Aldgate tube station from a suicide bomber, 7 July 2005. Two other underground trains near Edgware Road and Russell Square stations were similarly damaged, all within a few minutes of each other, followed a little while later by a bus in Tavistock Square.

Examining the bomb-damaged car of Benazir Bhutto in Pakistan, 2008.

Above. A sandstorm in Afghanistan, 2010.

Below. Giving a training-course in explosives to recent recruits to the FEL.

example of exactly that – a super-efficient detonation that had left no clues to its key ingredients.

But I was more curious. Perhaps I was simply less stressed than she was – I would have classed my workload as severe, but hers, as the most experienced case officer, was simply enormous – and I probably had a little more time to be curious. I found it hard to believe that a bomb of that size and scale of destruction could defeat us in that way. Having been to the scene at Kensington Palace Gardens, I also knew there were plenty of perfectly adequate receptor surfaces where we should be able to pick up chemical residue that could point to the type of device that had been used.

On my own initiative, I decided to conduct a second test, screening our samples from the cars, and from undamaged ones of similar vintage for comparison. This time I was looking for inorganic explosive material. It was then that I got close, almost without realising it, to what the Palestinians had been up to. That screen showed that, on sections of bodywork from both cars, there were large deposits of sodium chloride, otherwise known as salt.

'Hmm,' I thought, 'that's interesting.'

If it had been winter, I would probably have dismissed this as just a result of salt spreading on the roads. But it wasn't winter – it was high summer. On a few pieces of the Finchley car – the Triumph Acclaim – I also found some very small amounts of sodium *chlorate*, a quite different material to sodium chloride, that can be used in bombs when mixed with a fuel like diesel. The really interesting bit is that when sodium chlorate – available in garden centres in the form of weed killer – reacts in an explosion, it produces, as a by-product, you've guessed it . . . salt.

My results suggested to me that the main charge in both bombs might well have been one containing sodium chlorate, but I had nothing like conclusive proof. This was quite a far-fetched idea. Sodium chlorate had never been used as a main ingredient in a high-explosive bomb in Britain before. We had seen it lots of times in small pipe bombs or incendiary devices planted by the IRA, but almost never as the main charge in a bomb. One reason for this was that buying large quantities of weed killer was much harder to do without drawing attention to yourself than, for example, buying ammonium nitrate – the IRA's favourite main ingredient – which is bought and sold in huge consignments as fertiliser.

If sodium chlorate seemed unlikely, I also had no idea what had been used to detonate the main charge, whether it was sodium chlorate or not. Looking back, I can see that I was getting warm on this one and perhaps, if we hadn't both been under such pressure with other jobs, I would have pushed my theory harder. But, as it was, I was happy to follow Lisa's lead.

We both produced statements for the police about the two bombings that advanced the point they had been particularly effective detonations of high explosive that had left little or no residue for testing and analysis. My statement raised the possibility of sodium chlorate being the main ingredient but went no further than that.

Fast-forward a few months to January 1995 and the police made a number of arrests in connection with this case. The five suspects' hands, cars and homes were extensively swabbed for explosives residue. Lisa and I processed all the samples but again found nothing, apart from a statistically insignificant speck of RDX in a car belonging to a female suspect who was later released before trial.

The Israeli embassy bombing looked like it was heading for the 'inconclusive' file. But four months after the arrests, my theory on sodium chlorate received a major boost. In May 1995, ten months after the bombings, the police found a cache of bomb-making materials in a locker at a Nationwide Self-Storage facility near Heathrow. This had been rented by two of the suspects and it contained a large amount of partially- and fully-constructed IEDs in small tubs.

Alongside the chemicals and bombs there was also paperwork that included an invoice from a chemical company who had supplied the Palestinians with a large amount of sodium chlorate. This was still Lisa's case, and her own conclusions remained consistent with her own analysis of the bombs, but I took some satisfaction from realising that my curiosity had likely been leading me in the right direction.

This case may well have ended there as far as the forensics are concerned. But what happened next was pure theatre – in hindsight perhaps, a comedy of errors, all due to our facing something entirely new to the UK, though unrecognised at that point – but one that could so easily have ended in tragedy. At the Nationwide lock-up, the attending Met police EXPO examined the various completed IEDs. They each contained around 1kg of white powder into which were inserted photographic flashbulbs as initiators. His job was to make them safe, ready for transportation to the Fort, where they would be analysed and destroyed.

At that time in the UK, the only devices that had been seen in our line of work with flashbulbs as initiators were either incendiary devices or pipe bombs, where the main charge is tightly confined and would explode with just a flame, as opposed to a detonator. The most common ingredients for such devices were our old friend sodium chlorate – or weed killer powder – mixed with sugar.

In this instance the EXPO looked at the white powder and assumed that that was what he was seeing – a classic incendiary device, albeit quite a big one, made with weed killer and sugar. He knew that if he pulled the flashbulb out, the powder on its own would be harmless and could be transported without risk back to the FEL. But he was wrong.

The IEDs were duly packed up and placed in a police van that was then driven round the M25 towards Seven-oaks and on to the Fort. What neither the driver nor the EXPO who had given him the material knew was that, if the van had been involved in a violent braking incident or a crash, there could have been a major explosion.

It just so happened that when the police arrived at our reception, I was the on-call duty officer ready to receive and assess any new explosives material that was brought in. In those days – and it is hard to believe that we operated in such a manner – new deliveries, in whatever receptacles they had been placed into, were simply carried into the large reception room at the Fort, where a receptionist and a police liaison officer were present. (Partly as a result of what happened next, these procedures were radically changed and nowadays this all happens in an empty build-ing located well away from the main offices of the FEL, so that any unexpected detonation will cause minimum casualties and damage.)

I talked to the officers, who told me where the stuff had come from and the EXPO's view that it was sodium chlorate and sugar, which sounded highly likely. Then I opened the first sample bag and had a look inside one of the tubs. What I noticed was that the powder seemed uniform in its consistency. Normally, when sugar and weed killer are

153

mixed – even if caster sugar or icing sugar is used – you still see the granules of sugar, which stand out from the weed killer.

I wondered aloud if these bombers, whom we had not come across before, had simply worked their mixture into such a fine dust that spotting the constituent parts was much harder than normal.

Then I started thinking, what if this is not weed killer and sugar?

'I'm not sure about this stuff,' I said to the policemen. 'I think the best course is for me to try a burn test just to confirm that this is what we think it is.'

In the ordinary way, a weed killer and sugar mix would burn, and burn fiercely, like a roman candle, but without exploding when exposed to flame, so I had very little concern that anything else would happen. On my way to the lab I picked up a couple of trainees who were interested to see the process and we duly assembled around the old fume cupboard, an armoured box with forced ventilation to take smoke away and a reinforced glass door around which I could access the protected area with my arm. While it has very strong sides, the cupboard had a thin, non-rigid roof. Should a sample generate a significant blast, this was designed to flex upwards to absorb the explosive energy harmlessly. It was an indication of how rare that sort of eventuality was that the roof of the cupboard was littered with old aluminium sample trays and other bits and bobs.

Israeli embassy: something we had never seen before

In those days there were no set rules on the size of a sample used in a flame test – nowadays the process is mandated to start with an amount of powder equivalent to half a pea. I probably had a sample size of three or four peas, on a long-handled spoon, which I extended into the cupboard over a Bunsen burner flame. To say there was a loud 'bang' would not be quite correct. It was more of *whoomf!* as the material on the spoon ignited with sufficient force to create a blast wave that extinguished the flame – in itself quite hard to do – and then impacted the roof, flexing it violently enough to send the sample trays flying off the top and clattering on to the lab floor. I stood there stunned, feeling a little bit like a cartoon character who has just been blown up by his own bomb, with – figuratively – smoke coming out of my ears and my clothes in tatters.

The trainees were impressed; in fact we all started laughing.

'Bloody hell. Well, that's certainly not what I thought it was,' I told them. 'We need to find out exactly what this is . . . and fast.'

A subsequent series of chemical tests that we carried out immediately revealed the white powder to be triacetone triperoxide or TATP, a highly unstable explosive that is sensitive to heat, shock and friction and that we had never seen before at the Fort. It was subsequently used by the 'Shoe Bomber', Richard Reid, in 2001 and by the 21/7 would-be suicide bombers in London in 2005, and has been used in several major terrorist attacks around the world since then.

TATP is not something you can buy off the shelf. You have to mix it up yourself and it is made from the chemical reaction of acetone, hydrogen peroxide and a small amount of acid – for example, battery acid from a car. At that time we had no evidence of Palestinian bomb-makers using TATP in Europe, but they used it in the Middle East in detonators. The IRA never went that route because they were far more concerned than Palestinian terrorists about staying alive and TATP was regarded as too dangerous for them to use.

Once we realised what was in the packages in reception, we had the whole place cleared and then the tubs were carefully removed by staff wearing bomb disposal suits. They were taken to the high explosives area of the Fort, where the TATP was disposed of by dissolving it in many litres of acetone.

However, the discovery enabled me to finally piece together, in my mind at least, how the devices that had blown up at the embassy and at Finchley road were made. I believe the main explosive material was sodium chlorate (weed killer), probably placed in a large plastic tub and then mixed with a fuel of some kind – possibly diesel. Then a smaller tub of TATP would have been inserted into the main mix, into which a photographic flash bulb was inserted, connected to a battery and timer, which acted as the detonator. It would have been a highly effective – and, to our eyes, unusual – construction.

The case highlighted not only how potentially dangerous our procedures were at the Fort for receiving new material, but also the need for constant vigilance in our line of work, where there was always the possibility of coming across some new or previously unseen threat.

In a fascinating late detail, a police exhibits officer told me many years later that he remembered being at the lock-up near Heathrow and thinking there was some strange kind of flooring in the facility. As they walked around, the floor would 'crackle' under their shoes, he told me. I told him what he was hearing and feeling were small explosions of TATP residue that had been spilled on the floor by the bomb-makers and that were detonating through the pressure and friction of footfall.

Ultimately this was Lisa's case and she stuck to her conclusion that while sodium chlorate can be used to make explosives, she had no information to suggest that had happened here. She was not wrong and it made no practical difference to the outcome of the trial, during which both Lisa and I gave evidence, when two suspects, Jawad Botmeh and Samar Alami, were convicted. For me, though, it was a reminder to stay curious for as long as you can – not always easy when under great workload pressure.

11

A choice between a cover-up and coming clean

My second foreign trip on behalf of the FEL – four years after my visit to the site of the Lauda Air crash in Thailand – featured the biggest crisis of my professional career. It was an episode that drove home to me a lesson for life – if you make a mistake, the worst thing you can do is try to cover it up.

It was in early 1995 that the FEL was asked by a parliamentary inquiry in Portugal to bring to bear what was already regarded as its world-class expertise in forensic analysis of explosives on a long-running case that lay at the heart of political and public life in Lisbon.

The case was the death fifteen years earlier, in December 1980, of the country's then prime minister, Francisco de Sá Carneiro, who was among seven people killed when a twin-engined Cessna 421A light aircraft crashed shortly after take-off from Lisbon airport.

Carneiro, then aged forty-six, and the country's first conservative prime minster, had been in office for less than a year. His death was a profound shock for a country that had only six years earlier thrown off the shackles of its military dictatorship. Those killed alongside Carneiro included his partner, Snu Abecassis, his defence minister, Adelino Amara, and Amara's wife, and both the pilots.

The crash immediately sparked rumours of an assassination, with conflicting theories that either Carneiro or Amara had been the prime target of a bomb placed on the eight-seater Cessna. These rumours were fuelled by eyewitness reports that there had been a loud explosion before the plane began its descent. But a joint investigation by Portuguese police and civil aviation officials found the crash was the result of engine failure.

That conclusion was widely disbelieved and the case has since been the subject of at least ten parliamentary inquiries, one of which, in 1995, invited the FEL to examine the wreckage of the plane to try to establish, once and for all, whether a bomb may have been placed on board.

My colleagues and I were about to play a walk-on part in a high-profile political drama in which we knew the eyes of the Portuguese media and parliament would be upon us. I remember, during the first of three trips we made to Lisbon, feeling that we needed to be on our A-game in everything we did, not least because, at the end of our investigation, we would have to present our findings to the parliamentary inquiry in person.

EXPLOSIVE

The team selected for this tricky assignment consisted of me, as chemist, focusing on chemical residues, alongside our head of department, Allen Feraday, who would look for physical signs of explosives damage. We were accompanied by a young casework officer, Steven Watson, for whom this would be a valuable learning experience.

Our first trip to Lisbon was an exploratory visit, and we were hosted by Vincenzo Lopez (not his real name), a charming and fluent English-speaking police liaison officer. We attended a series of meetings with officials, who briefed us on the findings of earlier inquiries into the crash and the scope of the current one, which included the exhumation of the bodies for further examination. And we visited the hangar at the airport where the wreckage of the plane was stored, but we did not carry out an examination at that stage. It consisted of some quite large sections of the wings and fuselage and many smaller pieces of mangled aluminium, barely recognisable as parts of an aircraft.

A few weeks later we were back, ready to start work. Although it had been fifteen years since the plane had come down in a fireball, crashing into houses in the Lisbon suburb of Camarate, we knew it was still possible for explosive residues to be detectable. High explosive compounds like RDX and PETN, for example, can survive for up to twenty years if – and it's a big if – they are left undisturbed. As far as Allen's side of it was concerned, there was every likelihood that pitting caused by explosive impacts or metal showing signs of sheer forces could still be identified, even if rust had begun to form on broken edges.

The remnants of the Cessna had been kept in a secure area and, although the Portuguese police had carried out their own examinations previously, we felt reasonably confident that this was not going to be a wild goose chase. Wearing our trademark white suits to prevent forensic contamination and neoprene gloves, we began, under Allen's direction, looking for signs of physical bomb damage among the pieces of plane laid out on the floor. Initially we looked for what we called gross damage – distortion and fractures that could be caused by an explosive charge – and then narrowed our search to smaller physical evidence, particularly pitting.

Then Steven and I got to work swabbing those areas we thought would be most suitable for explosives trace analysis, where there could be microscopic residues. We also swabbed patches of the floor, pillars of the hangar and anything else nearby that could possibly have contaminated the wreckage. We wanted to be absolutely certain that, if we found any explosives residue, it was on the plane and not from anywhere else.

Having finished our trace work, Allen then identified several small pieces of the fuselage that he wanted to take back to the Fort with us for examination under an electron microscope. After securing permission from our hosts, and under Allen's direction, we cut them out using hand cutters and placed them in forensic bags that were labelled and sealed.

We worked for two days in the hangar and then headed home fairly sceptical about our chances of finding anything. There had been no *Eureka!* moment. Sure enough, Steven and I carried out trace analysis at the lab, using the gas chromatograph on the samples we had selected, and found nothing. Allen, meanwhile, decided his examination of the small metal sections was inconclusive – there were areas with possible pitting but the minute indentations could also have been caused by rust.

It was at this point that we – and more specifically I – made a major error. Allen asked me to swab one of the metal pieces we had cut out, in which he was particularly interested, and then conduct a trace analysis to see if we could find any explosives chemical residues. I remember saying to him that I would have to swab the areas in the lab where he had been working to make sure there was no contamination of the sample from those surfaces first before carrying out the test.

But what did not occur to me was that the sample had not been extracted from the wreckage under trace standards of cleanliness. In other words, the cutting tool was not cleaned prior to use because at that point we were only extracting samples for physical examination, not chemical analysis. If we had known the sample was going to be chemically tested we would have used a tool that had been issued from the trace lab at the Fort and that had been cleaned using ultrasonic bath solvent and carried in a sealed bag.

The next day I came in to work early, eager to see the result of the test on the sample I had swabbed. It was dramatic. It showed that there were explosives traces on the metal with a complex pattern that included not just RDX but also TNT and DNT. After having seen nothing of significance up to this point, we were all excited that we had the beginnings of a breakthrough. Maybe a bomb had been involved after all?

The next step was to write up a report on our findings and then send that to the Portuguese authorities, informing them that we would now follow up our initial screen or test with a secondary procedure to confirm the presence of the chemicals. With the report written, the procedure was duly carried out and it confirmed our findings; there was no doubt that this section of the fuselage was showing clear signs of explosives residue, a finding that was political dynamite in Portugal.

But there was something odd about this. The unusual combination of chemicals seemed hard to explain. I wondered what sort of bomb would include all those constituents? Would a bomb-maker really have used RDX *and* TNT *and* DNT? We were discussing it in the lab one afternoon when someone dropped the bombshell as it were.

'Hey, Cliff, can I just ask, how did you get this sample?'

'Oh, we . . . hang on . . . we cut it out.'

Then, almost to myself, I muttered out loud: 'And what did we cut it out with . . . oh fuck!'

Suddenly I realised the mistake we had made and my pulse quickened. We had a whole nation in Portugal to answer to and we had made a complete balls-up.

'Where is that cutting tool, because we need to swab it!'

The cutters were found and, lo and behold, the trace analysis produced an identical finding to the sample – that peculiar mix of RDX, TNT and DNT, no doubt harvested from a series of physical examinations in earlier cases.

I was furious with myself. How could I have been so stupid? When we were in the hangar we were operating on two standards or principles – physical examination and chemical – and yet back at the lab, in response to Allen's request, I had ignored the distinction and allowed a contaminated tool to dramatically change the course of our investigation.

I knew we were in serious reputational trouble and I took the problem home with me. I couldn't sleep, mulling it over in my head and imagining the ramifications in Portugal. We had given the inquiry information that indicated their prime minister had been assassinated and now we would have to own up to making a basic error in our procedures.

A choice between a cover-up and coming clean

Vanessa did her best to calm me down. She tried to tell me that it was a mistake anyone could have made, but, of course, I found that hard to accept.

But my assumption that we would be owning up to our shortcomings was not immediately shared by all my colleagues. When we all sat down to discuss what to do about it with Allen and more senior management, I found myself in a very awkward position. Someone suggested that we need not admit our error because we had not yet informed the Portuguese of the confirmation analysis. We could simply say to the inquiry that while the first test had indicated the presence of explosives, our follow-up had shown that not to be the case. That would be the end of the matter.

Except that it would not be the end of it. As I pointed out, our case files on all our investigations were available by law to our customers – in this case Portuguese parliamentarians – and to lawyers and the police. If we pretended the findings of the follow-up were negative, we would have to remove the paperwork showing the positive confirmation result and then conduct a second set of tests on blank samples and insert paperwork to support them. In short, it would be the beginning of a classic cover-up and none of us would be certain that we could control its consequences.

Deep down in my gut I knew I was going to have nothing to do with a cover-up. Partly it was my background, as the son of a policeman who had made his living by obeying the law, but mostly because of that mistake early in my adult life over red diesel that I vowed never to repeat. I would simply not entertain this. I told the group I would not be involved and that I would rather face the music in person in Lisbon than be party to what would have been a superficially attractive but completely wrong-headed face-saving exercise.

It was a stressful time. Allen's furious temper was always a lurking threat and, in the ordinary way, he might have lost it with me. But he knew that while I was prepared to carry the can for this, it was his investigation and, as such, he was heavily involved in the procedural error that we had made. Maybe wiser counsel would have prevailed anyway. Or, perhaps, because I spoke up so suddenly and vehemently that I would not entertain this, it made it easier for those tempted by the suggestion to take a step back and reconsider it. In any event, nothing more was said about it.

It was left for each of us to write his own part of the report. Allen wrote up his section of the report of our investigation for the inquiry and I wrote up mine, making it explicitly clear that we (and in particular I) had made a mistake.

'You know you'll have to answer for that, in front of the panel in Lisbon, don't you?' a senior manager told me.

'Yes. I don't care. I'll do it,' I said.

We flew to Lisbon for the third time. I sat on the plane in a state. I was imagining the Portuguese equivalent of

A choice between a cover-up and coming clean

Michael Mansfield, QC, preparing to take me and my report apart, sentence by sentence, watched by the assembled ranks of the media. My career – and the global reputation of the FEL – would be destroyed. I kept running it through in my head – what would I say, how would I frame it? But I knew there was going to be no way to sugar-coat this – I would just have to admit what had happened.

By this stage the apparently sensational findings of our work had been leaked to the media and in our hotel on the night of our arrival we were door-stepped by a TV crew, who found Allen and me sitting in the bar.

'So, Mr Ferady,' the reporter asked, 'you have found evidence of a bomb? Is that true? Do you believe our prime minister was murdered?'

Allen hated the media and had no plans to interact with them either in Britain or in Portugal and simply left the room and headed for the lavatory. That left me to fend for myself. I certainly wasn't going to run for it but I had no intention of making a dreadful situation even worse by talking to the media.

'So, there was a bomb?'

'You think the prime minster was murdered?'

'Look,' I said, 'I'm sorry, but I am forbidden to talk to you under the contract between your government and my organisation, which says I cannot talk to the media. Even if I wanted to, I am not allowed to talk.'

EXPLOSIVE

There was a little more back and forth, but eventually the crew realised they were not going to persuade me to say anything.

The next morning, with butterflies in my stomach, I skipped breakfast and went to what I was imagining would be the 'Portuguese Inquisition'. The inquiry was sitting in a grand building with three members of its panel ready to question both me and Allen, who went first. He told them that no clear evidence of explosives damage had been found on the samples we had taken.

Then it was my turn. I told the inquiry that initially we had found nothing through trace analysis, then we thought we had found evidence of complex explosives traces and then realised we had contaminated that sample with a 'dirty' cutting tool. In conclusion we could confidently say we had found no explosives traces. The first member of the panel then questioned me quite harmlessly, just checking a couple of details, and then the other two followed suit – they were also very polite. I was astonished.

When it was all over and we were walking out, I turned to Vincenzo, who had acted as our translator at the hearing.

'Vincenzo, what on earth went on there?' I asked him. 'Did they not understand about our screw-up? Did they realise what I was saying?'

Vincenzo just laughed.

'Of course they understood,' he said. 'They just couldn't believe that you had appeared in front of them and admitted all that in public – when you didn't have to! That would never have happened with Portuguese officials and they were seriously impressed.'

It seemed we had got away with far less damage to our collective reputation than I, and everyone else at the Fort, had feared. I have since used this story many times when talking to new recruits to the service to remind them that, if you do make a mistake – and we all do – it is far better to own up than try to cover it up. The consequences of admitting a mistake can sometimes surprise you.

The error we made reflected the developing awareness among us all at the Fort of the need for ever-more detailed protocols to deal with the problem of contamination and the operation of the trace lab. A year after our last visit to Portugal, this issue became headline news when it was discovered that a centrifuge in the trace lab had not been properly cleaned when the lab was moved several years earlier and was contaminated with RDX. Again this was a case where we reported on this mistake ourselves – in this instance to the Home Office, which was our main customer.

The upshot was the possibility that the outcome of scores of cases – many of them high-profile criminal trials – were now unsafe. The government appointed Professor Brian Caddy of Strathclyde University, a professor of forensic science, to examine over 100 cases where RDX had been found. He narrowed that down to fourteen trials where RDX had been detected and where that evidence had been used in court to help secure a conviction. But in each case he found the outcome of the trials should not be overturned.

The Caddy Inquiry, however, was a watershed in the way we operated at the Fort. His report made a series of detailed recommendations about how the trace lab should operate and about other procedures at the Fort, and during my time there the protocols became far more thorough and detailed.

In the old days, if you wanted to go to the trace lab, you just put an overall and some gloves on and walked straight in. By the time I left the FEL in 2013, there was a written procedure for going into the lab, which alone took about ten minutes to complete. Then there were very strict rules on how you changed your clothes and washed your hands before you were allowed to walk through the door.

Portugal was, in many ways, a coming of age for me. I had stood my ground against some of my own bosses and been vindicated, not that I took any pleasure in having had to do that. What's more I still had a job and I was loving it.

12

The Björk stalker – a weird interlude
with no explosives involved

Every career in forensic explosives investigation, which necessarily deals with an underworld of criminal or eccentric behaviour, has its weird episodes and the case of the Björk stalker was the outstanding one of mine.

And uniquely in my time at the FEL, there was, in fact, no explosive involved in the case. But it required me to watch a video in which a bright young man effectively disintegrated as a rational human being and then shot himself. Fortunately that final bit was mostly out of view, but it was not a pleasant experience and was something that has stayed with me ever since.

This was the case of Ricardo López, who became notorious as the stalker of the eccentric Icelandic pop star Björk in the mid-1990s. A 21-year-old from a middle-class family in Uruguay that had emigrated to the United States, López had become a recluse in his teenage years and seen his dreams of becoming a great artist dissolve in psychotic episodes of self-hate and chronic insecurity.

While working part-time for his brother's pest control business in Hollywood, he became obsessed with various celebrities and, three years before his death in September 1996, had developed a fixation about Björk. He followed her career intently, wrote her endless fan letters and even fantasised about inventing a time machine so he could befriend her as a child.

This was strange and unhealthy behaviour but not necessarily sinister. That changed when he read an article about Björk that revealed she was in a romantic relationship with a musician called Goldie. From that moment on López determined that she would have to be punished for this perceived betrayal and he started thinking about harming her with a device of some kind.

Over the last nine months of his life, he chronicled his descent into rambling suicidal madness in a twenty-two-hour video diary shot at his apartment in Hollywood. It was not clear whether he intended to kill Björk or, more likely, inflict injuries on her that would permanently influence the course of the rest of her life, satisfying a warped desire for his life to have an effect on hers.

To start with, López considered constructing a bomb filled with hypodermic needles containing HIV-infected blood, but realised that that would be very difficult to assemble.

Instead he designed his own variation on a letter bomb. It consisted of a hollowed-out book in which he placed a bottle containing sulphuric acid. This was connected to a mechanical trigger device that would cause the bottle to explode once the book had been opened. His plan was to mail this to Björk at her address in London and then kill himself.

And that is exactly what he did. Four days afterwards, he shot himself in the head with a .38 calibre revolver. The police in Hollywood were called to his apartment because of the smell and discovered his decomposing corpse.

On the walls López had scrawled a message to them pointing out that the stack of video tapes next to his camera chronicled an act of terrorism that would be of interest to the FBI. After officers had been through the tapes and watched López constructing the letter bomb, they alerted Scotland Yard, who intercepted the package at the Nine Elms sorting office in south London. The officers reckoned that they had only one day to spare before it was delivered, although it is likely it would have been vetted by Björk's management office first.

An EXPO was called and, having been briefed by the Americans that this was likely to be a device containing some form of acid, he decided to remotely disable it using a shotgun-type weapon. This fired a cartridge containing a slug of water that was powerful enough to smash the package apart and disable the device before it could trigger itself.

EXPLOSIVE

Inspecting the debris, he noticed that a caustic liquid had soaked some of the components and burnt the paper edges of the book. There was also a broken plastic bottle with some of the liquid still in it, which he carefully drained into a small plastic vial. Then he packaged everything up and sent it to me with a warning note attached: 'Be careful of the liquid!'

So there I was at a laboratory bench in the FEL with the handiwork of Ricardo López in front of me – a 'bomb', which, on the video, you can see him assembling while wearing few clothes and a protective gown, face mask and heavy rubber gloves. Although he would kill himself not long afterwards, he is heard at one point worrying about the dangerous effects of fumes from the acid when he first started working with it.

I needed to confirm exactly what this liquid was. A quick test with some pH paper that turns different colours according to whether it is dipped in acid, neutral or alkaline solutions, showed it to be extremely acidic. A few tests later, I confirmed that it was in fact concentrated sulphuric acid. Suitably protected, I then turned to the rest of the debris.

There were the remains of a printed circuit board, a tiny battery, some wires and some card that looked like it had all come from an electric birthday card that plays a message on opening. All the writing on it had been obliterated by the acid but it was clear that it was not part of the main device and was obviously intended to be opened first.

The device had been buried inside the book and it was designed to work on a purely mechanical basis with no electrics involved. When you opened the book the movement of the cover activated a trigger arm that opened a valve on a small gas cylinder – the sort you might have found in an old Soda Stream drinks dispenser.

This fired pressurised carbon dioxide gas into the bottle, which contained quite a large amount of acid – certainly a few hundred millilitres. After a second or two the pressure inside the bottle would have reached the point where it would have exploded. This would have happened just as a curious and bemused recipient of this device would have moved their face closer to the mechanism to get a better look. The injuries would have been horrendous.

After looking at it for a while, I came to the conclusion that this was a viable contraption that probably would have worked if it had got through. In my preliminary report to the police, I noted: 'I have not so far found any evidence of any actual explosive components, the device apparently being designed simply to shower anyone opening it with concentrated acid, which would be likely to cause serious injury to any such person, especially to exposed areas of skin and the face.'

A day or so later the police sent me a copy of a two-hour video that they had received from their colleagues in California and asked me to look at it. Although López was dead, law enforcement on both sides of the Atlantic were keen to establish that he had no co-conspirators and whether there was any residual threat to Björk or anyone else that we were not aware of.

I sat through the bizarre last moments of López's life watching him go from relative sanity to a naked figure with a shaved head, with red, black and green warpaint on his face, who picks up a revolver in front of the camera.

'I feel a little nervous now. I'm definitely not drunk. I am not depressed. I know exactly what I am doing. It is cocked back. It's ready to roll,' he said.

Towards the end the camera is pointing at the top half of López's head so that he is largely out of shot. As the Björk song 'I Remember You' finishes playing in the background, he is heard to shout: 'This is for you!' A round is fired, López groans and the chair that he was sitting on tips over. The camera is left lingering on a sign propped up on the back of his sofa that says, in hand-painted black lettering on a white background: 'The best of me. Sept. 12.' Police in California believed he had intended to spray this with his own brain matter, but missed.

It *was* weird – in my notes at the time I described the video as 'long and quite bizarre, unsettling even'. It was sad to watch someone fall apart and I was amazed to discover, while researching this book, that parts of the video had been released by the FBI and are now available on YouTube.

The Björk stalker – a weird interlude

Quite why anyone would want to watch it – other than psychiatrists – is beyond me.

The case promptly fizzled out after I had delivered my preliminary report to the police, after which the investigation was shut down. In the file I marked it 'NFA', meaning 'no further action', and then put the paperwork into the archive. But I kept the video in my office, not wanting someone to come across it in the archive and start watching it without realising what it was about or what happens at the end.

When I left the FEL, I handed it to my successor and recommended she destroy it, on the basis that it would not improve her life, and once seen she wouldn't be able to unsee it. It's all rather academic now, given that the same material is available on the internet.

Björk herself was understandably distressed by this whole business but still sent a card of condolences and flowers to the López family, which I thought was an impressive gesture. 'It's terrible, very terrible. It's a very sad thing that someone would shoot his face off,' she said shortly after this bleak drama had played itself out. 'I make music, but in other terms, you know, people shouldn't take me too literally and get involved in my personal life.'

Looking back on this story, it struck me that Ricardo López was unique in my experience in another respect. Of all the hundreds of bomb-makers I came across at the FEL, he was the only one that I actually saw going about his business, even if there was no conventional explosive involved and he was, by that point, already dead. In other cases I imagined how and where bomb-makers might have put their devices together, but I never saw it happen; in this case it was all there to see. Nevertheless, it was watching his descent from relative sanity into a total loss of reality that I have never forgotten, and probably never will.

13

The art of the pipe bomb

Most of the more effective improvised bombs that I came across during my years at the FEL involved a certain level of sophistication with both chemicals and electronics that ensured that they would work as designed. Most of them were fairly crude in their manufacture and appearance, with the emphasis on function rather than form.

The pipe bombs built by Jonathan Wilkes were of a different order. In fact I would go as far as to say that, certainly in terms of small-scale devices, they were the most accomplished pieces of work I ever came across. It was not just the use of chemicals and electronics that impressed, but the architecture and packaging of the devices that put them in a class of their own.

What is more, they were effective, even if they were never used in anger. I had no doubt that they were capable of killing or maiming lots of people, had one of them gone off in a crowded space like a pub bar. The effect would have been similar to the detonation of a powerful hand grenade, with shrapnel tearing into flesh and bone.

EXPLOSIVE

This particular case came about in October 2000, three years after I had been appointed a somewhat reluctant head of casework at the FEL on the retirement of Allen Feraday. I had never been particularly ambitious and never imagined I would lead the department I had joined a decade earlier, but, with Allen's career coming to an end, I was the most experienced person left behind.

I took on the role after discussing it with Vanessa, who pointed out that I would much rather run things myself than have to report to someone who was less experienced than I was. I knew that I would be doing less casework and more management, which did not appeal to me, but I secured an undertaking from my bosses – that was largely honoured – that they would leave me free to make decisions about casework in the best interests of our investigations and without constantly having to refer upwards. Little could I have known that my tenure would include the busiest times in the history of the FEL, when al-Qaeda-inspired Islamic extremists launched a string of major and planned attacks in the first decade of the new century.

Wilkes's elaborate bomb making was discovered when a gamekeeper, out and about in rural Gloucestershire near the hamlet of Syreford, happened upon a two-litre plastic water bottle sitting on top of a drystone wall. There were two pieces of MDF wood wedged on either side of it. On closer inspection the gamekeeper could see enough inside the bottle – wires and hundreds of stainless steel nuts – to realise that this was not something he should attempt to pick up.

Police were called and they duly summoned an EOD technician. What the gamekeeper had stumbled upon was the set-up for an explosives test using what we referred to as 'witness plates'. These were the two pieces of MDF, but they could have been bits of metal or hardboard, depending on the purpose of the test. The idea is to detonate a device and then examine the witness plates to assess how effective a bomb had been. In this case, were the sections of MDF heavily indented with buried nuts or had they been blown to pieces or had the nuts merely bounced off them? Either way, this test had been set up by somebody but not carried out.

After examining the bottle visually, the EOD used a remotely operated tool to shoot the top off it where he could see the command part of the device was located – the electronics, batteries and timer and so on. The various pieces that were left were then packaged up and delivered to the FEL, where I was ready to receive them. I could tell immediately from the fragments and the less-damaged parts that this was an unusually sophisticated pipe bomb. It had been made all the more potent by the addition of around 3kg of nuts and bolts surrounding the central charge.

I was intrigued to see how the whole device might have looked and assumed that that might be as far as we would ever get with this particular bomb-maker. But in an extraordinary coincidence five days later, another eight pipe bombs in identical plastic bottles were found by someone walking their dog in a wooded area near the village of Freeland in Oxfordshire, about 30 miles east of Syreford. It appeared that these ones had been stored in the woods for use at a later date and were found in two plastic bags.

Once again an EOD operator was tasked to attend and, to start with, he tried to open up one of the bottles using a remote tool, only for it to detonate, destroying the device entirely. This was obviously not ideal from an evidence-gathering standpoint.

After this incident, I was called to attend and advised the EOD contingent – by now a six-strong team – on what we had found during our examination of the first device. We were already working on the assumption that all nine bombs could have been built by the same bomb-maker. From what I had told them of the structure of the Syreford device, they were able to see that the remaining seven were, in fact, each in two parts and had not been fully assembled. This enabled them, during a 48-hour operation, to move them safely out of the bags, separate them and then package them up for delivery to the FEL.

The art of the pipe bomb

So what does a fairly standard pipe bomb consist of? The power of these simple but effective devices is based on the confinement of explosive material inside a small section of pipe, which has the effect of amplifying its destructiveness. As used by the IRA in Northern Ireland, for example, pipe bombs would typically be based on a 6-inch length of 2-inch diameter steel pipe, which comes with screw-in end caps. The pipe would be packed with 4–8oz of a form of smokeless propellant, which is used in ammunition and can be bought at gun shops and is usually based on nitrocellulose as its main ingredient but can also be mixed with nitroglycerine. A hole would be drilled in one of the end caps, through which an igniter cord, often containing a variety of gunpowder, would be inserted into the explosive. This could then be lit and the bomb thrown at its target. The IRA also used long command wires attached to an electric match head to electrically initiate pipe bombs as their intended victims came into range.

The bombs at Freeland were based on the same principle as the IRA version but were far more elaborate. They used a smaller diameter section of copper heating pipe, probably 1-inch in diameter, which had brass caps at both ends, one of which had an igniter wire inserted through a drilled hole. Inside the pipe, which stood vertically in the lower half of the bottle, with the bottom end buried in a thin layer of putty, was about 2oz of a dark powder, which we identified as smokeless propellant. To make up for its smaller size, the power of the device was augmented with the tightly-packed nuts and bolts surrounding the pipe.

The top half of the bottle started with a base plate that was anchored in another layer of putty by four small wooden stakes that ensured the assembly above was stable. Electrical power was provided by a couple of AA batteries, which were connected to the igniter wire and also to a small analogue clock. This had been doctored so that the minute hand would come into contact with a tiny metal post – probably a small nail – completing the electrical circuit that would detonate the bomb.

Just like the IRA bomb at the Beck Theatre, these devices also included a fail-safe mechanism, with two switches fitted to the outside of the top part of the bottle, one of which armed the bomb while the other activated a small LED light bulb inside. If the bulb was lit, it indicated to the bomber that the timer had not been set or that the clock arm had, for some reason, completed the circuit, meaning the device would explode if an attempt was made to arm it.

The Freeland devices were not all identical. Some included anti-handling elements, with a mercury tilt switch added that would connect the arming circuit if the bottle was moved after being deployed. As if that was not elaborate enough, three of the bottles had a further level of sophistication and included a small servo-motor with a rotating arm that could be activated remotely by radio control. When the servo-motor started up, the arm began to turn and at some point in its arc it would connect the circuit just as the minute hand of the clock was designed to do. This, of course, enabled the bomber to watch from a safe distance as a victim, or victims, came into range. We had never seen anything like this before at the FEL.

As I mentioned at the outset, all of these components were extremely well packaged inside the bottles, but they also provided us with a treasure trove of forensic evidence. We took the bombs apart at the FEL and police forensic experts on fingerprints, fibres and DNA analysis pored all over them while officers on the hunt for a suspect had around forty different components to track down with suppliers. It was through this process that a most unlikely bomb-maker was identified.

Initially police had imagined they might be looking for someone with terrorist connections, or perhaps a lone extremist or someone with military expertise who could build complex devices with the degree of 'finesse', as they put it, that these devices demonstrated. But Wilkes, aged forty, was the son of a Worcestershire teacher, had a degree in computer science and had run a number of successful IT companies. He had worked in Paris, where he was earning more than £100,000 a year and where he had a French partner and a young son. Most improbably of all, he appeared to be a stalwart of his local community and had begun to train as a magistrate, and had even already sat in some cases.

Wilkes was linked to the bombs not just by forensic evidence and by contacts with suppliers, even though he had made purchases of components using false names and false mailbox addresses, but because he lived in Freeland. It also emerged that he was a keen shot and his knowledge of firearms was thought by officers to have helped him understand the practicalities of bomb-making.

To start with he denied having built the bombs and claimed he had been blackmailed over an affair he had had with a former colleague and that the blackmailer had ordered him to obtain the various components. However, when faced with the weight of evidence linking him to the bombs, he capitulated on the first morning of his trial and finally admitted that he had built them himself but claimed that he 'never intended to harm anyone'. At that stage he said he had planned to use them only to kill himself because of the pressure of being blackmailed.

Wilkes was never linked by police to any blackmail plot and nor did they find any evidence linking him to terrorist organisations or evidence that he harboured extremist political views. The prosecution at the trial came up with the motive that he had been intending to use the bombs to target a former lover's new boyfriend, but I never bought that.

In any event, he was convicted in January 2002 under the Explosive Substances Act 1883 of possessing eight devices with intent to endanger life and of possessing the single bomb found at Syreford. Sentencing him to five years, Judge Peter Crawford, QC, told Wilkes, who never disclosed his real intentions or motivation: 'You are a man of education and intelligence. The devices were specifically designed to maim and kill. Who was the intended victim nobody can know for sure. It is a sad day when the court has to sentence a justice of the peace for a crime of this gravity.'

I thought the sentence was ludicrously light given the sophistication and destructive power of the bombs and the intent shown by Wilkes. It was ridiculous to suggest he was building these devices to kill himself or even another individual. It was quite clear to me – and to the police officers investigating the case – that he had built multiple bombs that he intended to deploy in a way that would cause multiple casualties.

The prosecution shared my frustration at the sentence handed down and, three months after the trial, the Court of Appeal in London extended his term to nine years. My belief that the bombs were intended to cause mass casualties – for example, in a pub or at a large public event (the police speculated that the Notting Hill Carnival may have been Wilkes's target) – was only reinforced when a month after the trial a man living near Wilkes, David Tovey, was arrested for writing racist graffiti.

Tovey's house was then searched. Police found guns and a great deal of bomb-making equipment, including PE4 military-grade plastic explosive, lead azide primary explosive for detonators, metal tubes scored so that they would shatter effectively in pipe bombs, plastic water bottles cut and prepared in the same way as Wilkes had done, explosive propellant and radio-control equipment.

It emerged that Tovey had attended Wilkes's trial, was a member of the same gun club as Wilkes and lived just two miles from him. Tovey got eight years for gun and explosives offences and three more for racist graffiti. It seems highly likely to me that he and Wilkes were up to something together, though such a connection was never established.

For the purposes of the trial we created a replica of Wilkes's pipe bomb without any explosives in it that showed the pipe with the nuts partly cleared out so the internal structure was easy to see. I remember looking at it and thinking, again, what a remarkably polished example of a pipe bomb this was. At the original trial, the prosecution had described his bombs as 'truly terrifying in their potential to maim or kill'. It was a view I wholeheartedly agreed with.

14

Operation First Strike

I was peering into a cupboard under the stairs in a small terraced-house in inner city Birmingham. Outside, it was a cold November morning in 2000, but I could feel a bead of sweat trickling down the back of my neck.

It was gloomy even though the light from the kitchen was partially illuminating the few tins on the shelves. But it was not the tins of food that had caught my eye.

Standing alone on the top shelf were two 'stay-fresh' plastic circular containers, each about five inches tall, identical save for the fact that one was green, the other yellow. Their lids were held down by wire clips.

I had good reasons to suspect that these might not contain food – say sugar or flour – but a highly dangerous primary explosive, one so volatile that it has never been manufactured commercially.

HMTD, or hexamethylene triperoxide diamine, to give it its full name, is, however, of use to terrorists looking for something combustible and violent for use in detonators.

I turned to Susan (not her real name), a junior FEL case officer, and could see that she was looking at the containers with the same thought in her head. Behind her a police officer who was accompanying us had his notebook in hand and was scribbling away.

'We're gonna have to find out what's in those,' I said to Susan quietly.

'Yes, Cliff, but shouldn't we get the bomb disposal guy in to deal with them?'

Outside the house – which was cordoned off – an EOD technician was waiting in all his kit with his wagon. But, unusually, it had been agreed between all the units on scene that day in the Sparkhill area of Birmingham, that Susan and I should do the first search of Moinul Abedin's rented terraced house.

The reason? We had no idea whether we would find actual bomb-making materials and equipment in the house or just traces of chemicals. If it was the latter, the danger of the EOD doing the search was that he could contaminate the house with residues from previous operations and the defence at a future trial would seize on that and have all the trace evidence dismissed.

We also knew that, if the EOD dealt with the containers, his operational protocols would probably require him to use a robot, or a special apparatus he had to shoot off the clips. The chances were the material inside would be destroyed in the process and we needed it to be recovered intact. We knew there were safety risks if we went in first, but we assessed them carefully, weighed them against the other factors and we all agreed on the decision we should go in first, continuing to assess the risks carefully as matters developed inside the property.

So we were first in on a case that would become the first in Britain to deal with an al-Qaeda-influenced Islamic extremist bomber. And we were not wearing the kind of protective gear that the EOD is equipped with; Susan and I had our flimsy white forensic suits on, latex gloves and Perspex masks, but nothing to help prevent serious injury in the event of even a small explosion.

'Look,' I said, 'if we can get into them and find HMTD, then the EOD can come in and carry out the rest of the search. The preservation of trace evidence will become irrelevant.'

'Yes, but if that *is* HMTD in there, Cliff, it could go up just from the action of opening the seals on the lids and you could lose fingers or a hand just like that.'

Our job does not require bravery in my opinion, but it does require a certain preparedness to take calculated risks. I had seen enough near misses to be fully aware of how dangerous a wrong decision taken in the heat of the moment could be. When talking to young recruits to the FEL, I always made the point that risks could be taken, but they had to be weighed up carefully. I often used to say to them: 'There has not yet been the last ever explosives accident, so don't let it be you, because, if it's you, it's going to hurt.'

I reached up and carefully picked up the green container. I could feel its weight and immediately felt reassured that it was not full to the brim of whatever was inside it. Of course the danger with two rubber seals held down by wire clips, as Susan had pointed out, is that, however slowly and carefully you try to prise them open, there is still going to be a moment when the seals burst apart. In the back of my mind I was thinking there could be grains of HMTD trapped in the seals and the action of releasing them could be enough to set off an explosion that could then blow the whole container.

'No, it's clearly nowhere near full – that is not going to happen,' I thought to myself. 'Just do it.'

I considered the matter further for a while, but said nothing more about the pros and cons. Opening those two containers would not only clear up the search issue with the EOD, but could potentially lead to the preservation of crucial evidence of a bomb-maker's intent found inside the home he was renting. In this case, I believed, there were good reasons to take what I judged to be a small risk – fully aware that, if I was wrong, it was me that would be hurt, something I was very keen to avoid.

I asked Susan to step back into the front room with the police officer and placed the container on a kitchen worktop nearby. I adjusted my mask to ensure my eyes were at least covered on both sides and then placed my hands firmly on each of the clips, right and left. Then, applying pressure upwards and evenly with my index fingers, I eased the clips slowly up until I reached the point of no return. I could feel my heart rate increasing slightly as their movement began to accelerate.

'Pop!' They both sprang open together and all was peace and tranquillity. I took a deep breath.

'There we go,' I said, trying to sound as nonchalant as possible as I lifted the lid.

Susan stepped forward and we both peered inside. The powder in the container was held in a small plastic bag, with a flimsy white drawstring pulled tight and knotted to close it at the top. I picked it up by the knotted ends, held between the thumb and middle finger of my right hand, and placed it on the worktop. Then I took a scalpel and cut into the bag to reveal a fine white substance that was definitely not sugar or flour. The police officer moved forward to take photographs.

I could sense the excitement in Susan – she was still learning the job and would go on to become one of the FEL's most accomplished casework officers – and here we were together, having uncovered what could be critical evidence in a potentially important terrorist case.

'Okay, let's check this out,' I said.

Right there and then we carried out a 'burn test' on the

powder, placing a small amount on a spatula and applying heat underneath using a cigarette lighter. It ignited with an immediate bright orange flash, leaving no residue.

'Bingo!' I exclaimed.

This was undoubtedly a sensitive high explosive that we later confirmed was HMTD. In the second container, which the EOD dealt with, we found lead azide, a primary explosive also suitable for use in detonators. Elsewhere in the house the EOD found five detonators containing HMTD, protective clothing, tools and a quantity of sodium chlorate, familiar to us at the FEL from the Israeli embassy bombing in London in 1994. Outside in a bin bag, we found wiring, latex gloves, kitchen scales and other items that bore traces of HMTD.

The investigation of Moinul Abedin and his alleged accomplice, Faisal Mustafa, has since gone on to acquire far more significance than we perhaps realised at the time as the global threat from al-Qaeda grew. The 9/11 atrocity took place in New York the following year and then a series of Islamic extremist terrorist attacks followed in Britain, including the 7/7 bombings in London in 2005, but this was the first sign of al-Qaeda's intent.

The case was unusual for the FEL in many respects. Working directly with officers from MI5 was quite rare in itself; we had to develop the world's first trace analysis test for HMTD that would stand up in court, and we had to battle the peculiarities of legislation originally framed in 1875 in what was, ultimately, a failed bid to ensure Mustafa was convicted alongside Abedin.

'Operation First Strike' (not the real name), as the police and security services dubbed it, had started for us the day before. We were called to assist a fifteen-strong team of MI5 officers that had been carrying out surveillance on Abedin, whom they codenamed 'pivoting dancer', and Mustafa, 'molten lava', for some time. They were interested in a small lock-up at a business park not far from Sparkhill in the Tyseley area of Birmingham.

At this early stage I went along without Susan, whose case this would be, thinking this was probably another waste of our time and that we would find nothing. But I went alone because an MI5 call-out was rare and, as the person in charge of casework at the FEL, I felt I should keep abreast of what – if anything – was found, and planned to fully brief Susan later.

The rules of the warrant to search the lock-up meant I had to stand on the threshold of the small room that Abedin, twenty-seven and of Bangladeshi origin, had rented under an assumed name because I was not specifically named in the document. The MI5 team, who had linked Abedin to the facility via a mobile phone of his they had acquired, had broken in by picking the lock and had then started to search the various drawers, shelves and a filing cabinet.

Every now and again they would wander over to show me things and it was not long before I realised that we had stumbled upon a full-scale bomb factory, or at least the store for one. In the end it was estimated that there were up to 100kg of chemicals in that room and, fairly early on in the search, I became aware that much of it was components for HMTD.

You could tell immediately that this was a concerted operation. By that stage both Abedin, who had previously worked in an Indian restaurant and as a used-car salesman, and Mustafa were in custody. In a search of Mustafa's home in Stockport, the police found traces of HMTD and also material on his computer that the prosecution would claim amounted to a 'terrorist's handbook'. The files on the hard drive included titles such as 'Mujahedin explosives handbook' and 'Guerrilla arsenal: advanced techniques for making explosives and time-delay bombs.'

At the house in Sparkhill, officers also found what I believed to be an improvised explosives testing kit. This consisted of rolls of roofing lead and a frying pan. It appeared to have been used to conduct what we called the 'lead block test', when a sample of explosive material is placed inside a circular block of lead and then detonated. From the deformation of the lead you can then tell how potent the substance is likely to be. The frying pan in this case had a big dent in it.

Abedin tried to claim he and Mustafa were planning little more than a fireworks business. But he was more or less bang to rights, with police able to link him to the lock-up, the house, and even his local mosque, where explosives residues were also found. Mustafa, on the other hand, proved far more elusive. Aged thirty-eight and also of Bangladeshi origin, he had a degree in chemistry and a PhD in metal corrosion, and had been tried four years earlier for conspiring to cause explosions with two other men. He was acquitted on that charge but sentenced to four years for illegal possession of a pistol with intent to endanger life.

The problem in this case was that we could not link him with any bulk finds of explosives, only traces of HMTD.

Mustafa and Abedin were prosecuted at Birmingham Crown Court in early 2002 under an old statute, the Explosives Substances Act 1883, which makes it illegal to possess an explosive substance likely to cause danger to life. However, that act also refers to the even older Explosives Act 1875, which covers the manufacture of explosive substances and contains a loophole which Mustafa nimbly jumped through.

The 1875 Act allows anyone to manufacture less than 50g of any explosive, so long as they are doing so for experimentation and not for sale or for what the Act terms 'practical effect'. New anti-terrorist legislation is now on the statute book, but this ancient loophole still exists, although you now need what is called an 'Acquire and Keep' certificate from the police if harmless 'experimentation' is your intention.

To my mind this is absurd. No member of the general public should be able to make a primary explosive without a manufacturing licence and the new certification restriction is far from adequate.

If the legislative background was difficult, so was the issue of establishing a reliable test for traces of HMTD that would satisfy a court of law. Apart from one earlier uncontested case, we had not dealt with HMTD at all at the FEL, and as the trial of Abedin and Mustafa drew near, we had to work exceptionally fast to try to get up to speed. Testing bulk HMTD and demonstrating its chemical properties was no problem; trace analysis using liquid chromatography was far more chemically complex.

The normal procedure with a new substance is to research and establish a testing methodology and then write a formal paper setting it out. This is then published in a reputable journal and peer reviewed to ensure it is robust. In this case we did not have time for that, so we were reduced to writing an open letter, which was published in the *Journal of Forensic Sciences* without peer review. It was hardly adequate to the task, but it was the best we could do in the time available. It has, of course, since been properly published and peer-reviewed in the normal way.

It was down to Susan, who had precious little experience of what we termed 'contentious' cross-examination, to front up for us at the trial, and she stood up to an entire day in the box on the weaknesses or otherwise of our test and trace analysis for HMTD. I sat at the back of the court listening as she fended off one hostile question after another from the defence teams, and I felt for her. That night she was mentally exhausted. The following day, when the defence moved on to question her about sodium chlorate, which had been discovered in Abedin's home in various mixes with wax, sugar or sulphur, I sensed she was starting to hit the buffers.

During an adjournment the prosecuting QC, Colman Treacy, asked whether I would be prepared to go into the box in Susan's place and I jumped at the chance. I was determined that the prosecution evidence be presented in the best possible light, and I knew that my greater experience would help with this. It would also bring an end to the very stressful ordeal that Susan was having to endure.

The barrister for Abedin tried to suggest that I had no real idea whether sodium chlorate could work as an explosive with the various components added as fuel because I had, presumably, never tried to make a bomb of any kind using it. I was having none of it, having led numerous explosives courses for new recruits at the FEL where we did exactly that.

'Well, actually, I've made dozens and dozens of bombs with chlorate mixtures of all kinds and I do it regularly as part of the courses I do at the FEL,' I said. 'We also have detailed experience of analysing sodium chlorate as a component in improvised explosives from other cases in recent years. If I tell you that I know this or that mixture of sodium chlorate with another substance will explode if detonated sufficiently, you can take it that I know what I am talking about.'

I could see I had taken the wind out of his sails with one answer and from there it was more or less plain sailing.

But the difficulties we faced during the trial summed up what, for all of us, had been a hard grind on a complex case that involved multiple locations and many long meetings with police and legal counsel. For me personally, the detailed interest I took in the case alongside all my other responsibilities took a toll, something that was made infinitely worse by the death of my mother during the build-up to the trial.

She had been living alone in Mansfield after having divorced my father many years earlier and had had breast cancer that was treated with a mastectomy and chemotherapy. We all hoped and believed it had been nipped in the bud, but a few months after I first went up to Birmingham on this investigation, she returned from a holiday on a cruise ship feeling unwell with what she thought was flu.

Eventually it was discovered that her cancer had not only returned but had metastasized and spread to her liver. It was a desperate diagnosis and she went downhill very quickly and died just three months later. Each time I went up to the Midlands to work on the case I would take time off to visit her, and there is no doubt the strain of losing her combined with pressures from work took its toll.

I only discovered several years later that anyone had noticed when, during an FEL social evening shortly before I retired, a colleague mentioned to me that they had all been fully aware that I was losing my mother. She said everyone in the department had also noticed that I was struggling and that I had lost something of my normal upbeat mood as I co-ordinated the research and evidence in preparation for the case.

This episode will also never be forgotten for one final, bizarre reason. During the presentation of the defence case before Mr Justice Hughes at Birmingham Crown Court, the barrister for Abedin called to the witness box an independent forensic explosives scientist whom I knew quite well. I also knew that he was somewhat eccentric, but what happened next shocked even me.

During a recess in the hearing, he approached me outside the court.

'Hey, Cliff,' he offered

'How's it going?' I replied briskly.

'Guess what?'

'What?'

'Well, I've got some HMTD with me here in my briefcase and I am going to take it out and show it to the jury. You know, I will tell them that it's dangerous, but, as you and I know, it's not *that* dangerous, otherwise how could I have it with me in the box . . .'

'What? What did you say?' I replied, mixing astonishment and incredulity in equal measure. 'You've brought HMTD with you to court?'

'Yeah,' he said, 'it's a tiny sample in a vial, but that's all I need. There's no need to get worked up about it.'

'You just wait there,' I said, and marched off to find the nearest police officer.

I explained what was going on and the officer responded with what you might call due urgency, confiscating it from the hapless expert. In fact, an EOD operator was called to deal with it and there then followed a lengthy legal discussion between the judge and the lawyers about what to do with the witness. The lawyers were aided, I have to admit, by my furnishing them with my well-thumbed copy of the *Guide to the Explosives Act, 1875*, which they fell on like kids with a new toy.

Eventually a somewhat irate Mr Justice Hughes decided he would not make a ruling on whether the scientist had broken the law and the court returned to the business at hand with the rest of his much-delayed evidence. It was a remarkable example of irresponsible handling of highly dangerous explosive material by someone who should have known better.

The two suspects were originally charged with conspiracy to cause explosions to endanger life. In the end, while the jury found Mustafa not guilty, having evidently accepted that he had not known what Abedin had been up to, Abedin was sentenced to twenty years for activities that the judge said had the potential to kill or maim large numbers of people. 'This is a serious plot,' he told him. 'It was a plan to cause explosions on a scale which was likely to put lives in danger.'

15

A booby trap that got personal

In general I tried not to get personally involved in the cases I took on at the FEL. But there was the occasional exception that proved the rule and the torch bomb that maimed and blinded Stephen Menary in February 2001 in west London was a case in point.

There is nothing – nothing at all – that I can look back on about this case that gives me any satisfaction. In fact, the more I think about it, the less good I feel about it.

This was a booby trap attack that was never solved by the police – one negative. I made very little headway in determining where the components for the bomb had come from – another negative. I got emotionally, or temperamentally, involved – yet another negative. And, worst of all, the victim could not have been less deserving of his fate.

And that is why I crossed the line. When I heard what had happened to Stephen, I was angry, and, despite being in charge of all the casework that the FEL was undertaking at what was a busy time, I took this case on myself.

A booby trap that got personal

'F*** it, *I* will do it, and see if I can help the police find the bastards who did this,' I told a colleague.

Being angry or emotional is no state in which to conduct a forensic science investigation. Detachment, objectivity, patience and clear thinking are required and anger does not help in the application of any of those qualities. More likely an angry forensic investigator will rush to judgement, allow emotive factors to influence conclusions, and see pathways or links that were perhaps better left unconnected.

On 25 February 2001, Stephen – then aged fourteen – was on his way into a paratroop training session at a Territorial Army (TA) base in White City in west London, where he had served in the Army Cadet Force for a couple of years. His ambition was to join the army full-time when he was older.

At some point as he approached the base he spotted what looked like an army-issue hand torch – with green camouflage-style coating – lying on the ground. It was on the pavement or close to the door that he was about to enter. Thinking that someone had dropped it, Stephen picked it up and at that point his life changed for ever.

He either pressed the 'on' switch or, having done that and seen no light come on, began unscrewing the battery cap. The torch exploded in his left hand. The force of the detonation ripped the door he was entering through off its hinges. The damage to him was far worse. Stephen's chest and stomach were torn open by shrapnel, his left hand was severed at his lower forearm and he lost the sight of his left eye. He also suffered long-term damage to his hearing.

The iniquity of this really got to me because it turned out that, as a baby, Stephen had battled and survived a rare form of cancer that had destroyed the sight in his right eye. This explosion had thus rendered him completely blind. He spent six weeks in hospital, where he displayed remarkable stoicism in the face of what were horrific injuries, telling journalists he just wanted to get back to school as soon as possible. 'I do not feel that angry,' he said. 'In a way I am glad it was me, because if it was someone else smaller it may have been a lot worse.'

I did not go to the scene. It was small, relatively straight-forward and the anti-terrorist police officers knew exactly what they were doing. I remember sitting in the lab at the Fort and looking at what they recovered. Fragments of a green rubberised plastic torch, bits of battery, part of a press-stud connector for a battery that could not have been part of the original specification of the torch and a small piece of aluminium tube that looked like it could have been part of a detonator.

This was a small-scale attack but its ramifications were potentially enormous. It was followed by further attacks in London, including a bomb outside BBC Television Centre, not far from Stephen's TA base. The immediate finger of suspicion was pointed at dissident Irish republican terrorist groups, like the Real IRA or the Irish National Liberation Army, both of which had rejected the 1998 Good Friday Agreement. Was this, the police wondered, the beginning of a mainland bombing campaign in the run-up to the expected General Election (that returned a Labour government in June under Tony Blair)?

Officially – and behind the scenes too – the police were keeping an open mind. This was because officers had picked up rumours that perhaps Stephen had been injured in a prank or grudge that had gone disastrously wrong. I found that hard to believe or even consider as a likely explanation, but I was desperate to try to help make a breakthrough.

My examination of the debris enabled me to fairly quickly reach a broad understanding of what the bomb-maker had done. But, as was often the case with the work we did at the Fort, this was not enough to help the police in their search for a suspect. Forensic explosives science becomes much more useful once a suspect has been identified, when it can either help prove a case or work in the opposite direction.

This was a conventional torch – an American-style military model – that was normally powered by batteries in a carrier inside the body. These had been replaced by a quantity of plastic explosive with a detonator inserted into it. This was probably connected by wire to one side of the on/off switch, while the other wire ran into a PP3 nine volt battery – the sort you find in smoke alarms – via a press-stud connector. Press the 'on' switch and the circuit is completed, the detonator flashes and the whole thing goes up.

On some of the fragments of the torch I found traces of RDX and PETN, explosive compounds that are often – but not always – found in Semtex plastic explosive. This again pointed at Irish republican terrorists, who had been using Semtex for years. But I could not be sure it was Semtex. The PETN traces, for example, may well have come from the detonator.

The police, meanwhile, were insistent that I do my utmost to rule out British plastic explosive or plastic explosives that the British army used, so that they could eliminate the possibility of a prank or internal grudge.

One defining characteristic of plastic explosive used by the army is the presence in it of traces of lithium. But doing a test for lithium would mean almost all the fragments would have to be soaked and washed in a solvent, such as a mild acid solution, prior to that being injected into an ion chromatography machine. The process of doing this would destroy any fingerprint evidence left on the torch fragments. Conversely, if the fingerprint evidence was collected from the fragments prior to a lithium test, the treatment required in that process would make a lithium test impossible.

I agonised for days over whether to do a lithium test or not. What if the police found a suspect and we had no fingerprint evidence to match him or her with? Given the state of the bits of torch, viable fingerprint evidence seemed unlikely, though not impossible. I was sceptical about a prank or grudge, but, on the other hand, what if it turned out to be army issue explosive? The police would be handed a huge advance in their investigation. After mulling it over for the umpteenth time, I decided to do the test. It came up negative for lithium. I have to say I was angry. I had got nowhere and, in the end, the police got nowhere too.

This could have been a prank, or perhaps the torch was a tool in a vendetta that ended up in the wrong hands, but it seemed most likely to me an Irish terrorist operation, although I could never be sure. But once the lithium test had been done it was unlikely we would ever be able to link the debris with a suspect, either through fingerprints or the newly available techniques using DNA testing.

The feeling of dissatisfaction was lessened only by the fact that, in years since, I have used this case on training courses to drive home to people – especially soldiers serving in Afghanistan or other areas of conflict – never to try to operate a machine or device that you find lying in your path. It might be a small transistor radio or a torch, but the lesson is the same – do not switch it on or even pick it up.

The problem, of course, with a torch is that, once they find it, people feel an almost irresistible temptation to see if it works.

None of this is of any comfort to Stephen, who needs lifelong care, or to his mother, Carol. On his eighteenth birthday he was feted by Tony Blair, whose wife, Cherie, posed with Stephen on the steps of No. 10 Downing Street to acknowledge his bravery. But mostly it has been hard graft for him and I was shocked to read some years later that he and his mother even had to fight to achieve the full compensation he was due for his injuries.

16

The Bali nightclub bombings:
when experience counts

The scene of the biggest loss of life in a single terrorist incident that I attended was the Bali nightclub bombings of October 2002 and I will never forget visiting the morgue at the local hospital a few days after the attack.

Two bombs had destroyed and set fire to two nightclubs in the downtown area of Kuta Beach, just a stone's throw from the clear waters of the Pacific Ocean. They killed Australian and British tourists, local Indonesians and people of twenty other nationalities, and the morgue in the capital, Denpasar, was overwhelmed.

The facility at the Sanglah Hospital held a maximum of ten bodies but was having to deal with over 200 dead. Many of the bodies were burnt beyond recognition or had suffered severe trauma because of the sheer force of the main blast. Pathologists and volunteers were working around the clock to try to identify victims in tropical heat, and the lack of refrigeration was making their task all the more difficult.

EXPLOSIVE

I had been in Bali for a couple of days when I accepted an invitation to visit the morgue from the British coroner, Alison Thompson, who had gone out to the island to investigate the deaths of the twenty-eight Britons killed in the atrocity. I was accompanied by my colleague Sheila Collins, a gifted young casework officer at the FEL, and we arrived to find bodies wrapped in white sheets lying in an open courtyard.

They were arranged in two long lines and large bags of ice from the supermarket, with blue and red lettering on them, which would normally have been destined for the bars of downtown Kuta, had been placed between them at regular intervals. It was the best that the mortuary staff could do, but the corpses were putrefying and fragmenting in the heat.

I had seen bodies before in the course of my work, and would do again, but not on this scale. However, it was not the sight of the corpses that stayed with me afterwards; it was the quiet dignity of the local Balinese people who had turned up there searching for missing relatives. On the walls there were messages about the missing and heartfelt pleas for information, while, all around us, people stood silently – many wearing face masks to ward off the smell – waiting for the chance to pull back a sheet in the expectation, or perhaps dread, of recognising a loved one.

That morning at breakfast in our hotel I had shared a table with Dr Richard Shepherd, one of Britain's top forensic pathologists, who had flown out to help carry out post mortems on the victims, and we were discussing our plans for the day.

'So what have you got on this morning, Cliff?' he said to me as we sipped coffee and enjoyed croissants and fresh fruit.

'Oh, I expect we will be visiting the Indonesians' explosives lab in the centre of town to see some of the samples they have collected from the scene and then I'll probably spend some time writing up my report,' I said.

There was a pregnant pause while I came to the unavoidable conclusion that it would only be polite for me to return the question in the normal way, even if I dreaded the answer.

'And what about you, Richard? What are your plans today?'

'Well,' he said cheerfully, and with the enthusiasm of a true professional, 'I have more or less finished with the intact bodies and today I want to move on to deal with the individual body parts.'

'Right . . . yup,' I said, swallowing slowly and allowing the imagery that his answer provoked to sink in.

'Well, I hope it goes well,' I said, as I got up to leave.

'Yeah, thanks,' he replied.

My job could be gruesome at times, but it was nothing compared to what Richard had to contend with, and I found his upbeat mood and positivity utterly astonishing.

I thought about it again at the morgue as I watched him and other pathologists from various nations who had flown in to help carrying out their remarkable work in the most difficult of circumstances.

Not for the first time in my life, I was grateful for the fact that I have no sense of smell.

Actually, Richard was putting on brave face like everyone else in Bali during those difficult days. In his 2018 memoir, *Unnatural Causes*, he wrote of his experience there in a way that I can wholeheartedly identify with:

> It was a hard, exhausting and traumatic time. I have subsequently visited the memorials to this atrocity both in London and in Perth, Western Australia, but no memorial is necessary to remind me of the decaying bodies, the ice, the smell, the single dripping tap in the mortuary that was our water supply and the overarching sense of the futility of terrorism. I am not sure it has ever really left me.

We had gone to Bali as part of a British team led by officers from the Metropolitan Police's anti-terrorist branch, SO13. Our job was to help advise the Indonesian authorities and a team from the Australian Federal Police, who were working with them and were co-ordinating the international response to an attack that had shocked the world.

The trip had started with the usual row in Whitehall over which department should pay for our visit and, even as we got on the plane at Heathrow, I could sense the gloom that had spread from Kuta all the way around the world. There were only a few rather subdued looking holiday-makers on the flight, which was full of disaster professionals like myself, heading out to see if we could help.

I had read about the bombings in the papers and seen footage on television of the aftermath, which featured an inferno after the two nightclubs that were attacked – Paddy's Bar and the Sari Club – had been blown to smithereens. Apart from the dead, there were more than 200 people injured, many of them young people on world tours or Australian footballers celebrating the end of their season – and many of them had suffered terrible burns.

I knew this wasn't going to be a pleasant experience, but I didn't dwell on it too much. It may sound cold and uncaring, but I had grown inured to that aspect of the job. As I sat in business class heading east from London, I was thinking more about the technical challenge that lay ahead and what Sheila and I could do to help the Australians in particular, who would lead the investigation on account of having suffered the biggest loss of life among their nationals in the bombings. We knew that they had never had to deal with an incident on this scale, in what was the biggest single Islamic extremist outrage since 9/11 a year earlier, and it would tax their resources to the limit.

Seven days after the bombs had detonated, we arrived in the heat and humidity of Bali and went straight into a briefing with the Australians and with SO13 officers who had already been on the island for several days. This would prove an interesting experience for me on a professional level because I was immediately confronted with someone from another country doing a similar job to my own but who probably had far less experience of large vehicle bomb scenes than I had.

He was a member of the Australian delegation and was in the equivalent role to our bomb disposal technicians, what the Aussies call an 'EOD Tech'. He was under pressure to come up with an explanation for the media and for the governments concerned about what had happened late one night on Kuta's Legian Street, in what was known as the 'leisure capital' of the island, and he seemed to me to have been rather quick to have reached conclusions based on questionable evidence.

With the aid of diagrams on a whiteboard, he told us that there had been two vehicle-borne bombings that had followed an earlier explosion in Paddy's Bar. One of the vehicles had driven the wrong way up the one-way street outside the Sari Club opposite Paddy's Bar and blocked the traffic. The other then approached from the opposite direction and both had exploded, one with a far bigger charge than the other. He estimated the size of the main bomb to have been in the region of 150kg and that it consisted of an improvised mix of explosive and had ignited with what is termed 'a low-detonation velocity'.

The Bali nightclub bombings

I sat listening to what was a confident and apparently well joined-up explanation, much of it based on eye-witness accounts from locals and tourists, but, to me, it just seemed far too slick and comprehensive for that stage in the investigation. It seemed to leave nothing to be further explained and I found it difficult to accept, though I said very little to indicate my scepticism about what I was hearing.

I had a chat with him and sensed that he quickly realised that I knew a bit about bombs and explosives. He seemed to step a back a bit and go on the defensive; I could see that it was almost inevitably going to be his version of events against mine. We talked in particular about a computer program that he had used to estimate the weight of explosives in the main bomb. It relies on measuring the size of the crater a device causes. He had used this because there was a sizeable hole in the road outside the Sari Club.

But I had never trusted this methodology. It might be reasonably accurate if you know all your main parameters, such as what type of explosive has been used, how far off the ground a device detonated, the nature of the ground it had been planted on and so on. It is also very tricky to accurately measure where a crater starts and finishes – is it where the road is first cracked open? Or where the tarmac starts to turn down into the hole?

In my experience, the best way to measure the size of a bomb in an urban area is to walk away from the epicentre, noting broken widows until you reach the last broken glass likely to have been caused by the explosion and measure the distance from there to the crater. There are published tables relating distance in this way to the size of a bomb and, in my opinion, they produce far more reliable results than the computer program my Australian counterpart favoured.

In Bali I did try to use this technique, and walked outwards from the centre of the explosions on Legian Street past the rubble of the nearest buildings, checking on broken windows. But, in that setting, this method was not going to work satisfactorily, because there were often shutters in place of windows; where there were windows, they were almost always open because of the heat, and thus had not been shattered at the time of the incident.

My Australian colleague's conviction that it was a low-velocity explosion was interesting too. I had no idea if he was right, but I knew that it can be tricky to work out what sort of explosion has occurred by looking at the type of destruction caused, particularly with large blasts. The impact of a blast can be very uneven. There are, for example, focusing effects, which I had identified at the IRA bombing of St Mary Axe in the City of London in 1992. This occurs when a blast wave that follows the shock wave from an explosion hits a building and is then focused like the lens of a camera. It can bounce off one building and then hit another on the opposite side of the street and destroy it, while buildings adjacent to it are left untouched.

The Bali nightclub bombings

At the end of the meeting I thanked the Australians for their presentation and we all agreed that the best thing for all of us was to get to the scene first thing in the morning.

I slept fitfully, fighting jetlag, in a beautiful hotel a few miles down the coast from Kuta that had been selected for us by SO13, where Bali's charms were presented to stunning effect. My room was in its own chalet in the gardens, in amongst palm trees next to the beach, and with the warm water of the ocean lapping not far from my door.

The next morning – eight days after the bombing – Sheila and I headed to the scene, fearing that we would find, as I had at the Lauda Air crash in Thailand just over a decade earlier, that it had been turned into a scavenger's tip.

The place looked like a war zone but I had done the Indonesians a disservice; it had been well sealed off by police and, what's more, almost all the many vehicles that had been smashed up in the bombing had been left in situ, even if some had been moved to assist casualty evacuation and firefighting.

The area where the bombs had gone off was a low-rise part of town where lots of small boutiques and shops alternated with bars and nightclubs with thatched roofs on a narrow street. I was not surprised by the extent of the damage to the surrounding buildings and vehicles but immediately realised that my Australian counterpart was miles off with his estimate of only 150kg of explosive. This was a far bigger bomb – it would turn out, in my view, to be nearly ten times the size.

The first stop was Paddy's Bar, where it was clear from the damage at the seat of the explosion – the location and concentration of pitting on the walls and pillars of the building – that a device had been detonated at tabletop height. There was no crater in the floor and we could see that there was biological matter – flecks of human hair and skin – driven into the ceiling above what looked like the centre of the damage above the bar. Our Indonesian counterparts, led by a charming and ever-helpful forensic explosives scientist called Yusuf, had found traces of TNT near the seat of the explosion. There was little doubt or disagreement that this had been a suicide bombing. It later emerged it had been carried out by a man who was wearing a device concealed in a rucksack.

That bomb had been the first to detonate and it had prompted scores of people to rush out on to the street, where the second bomb then exploded outside the Sari Club about twenty seconds later, killing and injuring many of the people who had escaped from Paddy's Bar. I started to examine the scene outside the Sari Club and in particular a car that SO13 officers directed me to that they said the Australians believed had been driven by another suicide bomber. This was supposedly the car that had been driven the wrong way up the street and had then blocked the traffic.

The Bali nightclub bombings

The Australians had come to the conclusion a suicide bomber had been at the wheel because, although the roof of the car was squashed down, there was quite a neat dome shape in it, which, in their view, could only have been caused by the head of someone impacting it in the instant that his explosive vest detonated. But this was stretching credulity to the limit.

I looked at it and saw that the driver's seat was largely undamaged, the roof had not come off as you might expect if a bomb had gone off inside the vehicle, and there was no crater on the road underneath where the car had originally been found. Recovery teams had not found a body or body parts consistent with there having been a bomber in the car.

'You're telling me this is a suicide bomber's car and I am telling you there are all sorts of reasons why that is just wrong,' I told the SO13 officer who was accompanying me.

'That's what the Aussies are saying.'

'Well, their explanation fits nothing that I am looking at. I don't know why there is a dome in the roof but I am certain this car has not been damaged in a suicide detonation.'

Looking at the area outside the Sari Club, I found no evidence of two vehicle bombs having gone off either. There was one crater and the scene was consistent with just one van bomb – it turned out to be a Mitsubishi L300 – having gone off outside the club. There was no doubt in my mind that that vehicle had been parked or had come to rest before it exploded and that it was in line with the direction of the one-way traffic.

With almost all vehicle bombs you can tell which direction they were pointing at the point of detonation by where the engine and back end of the chassis end up. So long as the engine is in the front of the vehicle and the explosive is packed behind it, either in the seating area or the cargo bay, the effect of the explosion will be to throw the engine out in a forward direction, roughly in line with how the vehicle had been parked. In this case the engine block of the Mitsubishi was found on a roof in line with the van, while bits of the rear part of the van had been found by Yusuf and his team in line with the chassis behind it.

After a few hours at the scene I had reached my core conclusions about what had happened and, I believe, they helped to re-settle the investigation on the right track. Sheila and I swabbed some surfaces and we took those samples back to the FEL for testing. They showed the presence of potassium chlorate. This is similar to sodium chlorate, which may have been used in the bombing of the Israeli embassy in London in July 1994. In Asia, potassium chlorate is widely available and used in products such as disinfectant and soap and can be purchased in bulk. If it had been the main ingredient of the large bomb, we knew it would have been mixed with a fuel of some kind, but it was not until the trial of the perpetrators that we found out exactly what they had done.

The Bali nightclub bombings

During the hearings in 2003 that led to three members of the Jemaah Islamiyah extremist group being shot by firing squad in 2008, it was confirmed that the device outside the Sari Club had been detonated by a second suicide bomber. According to an account by one of the defendants, it consisted of 1,020kg of a mixture made up of potassium chlorate, aluminium powder (that is found in paint products) and sulphur. The mixture was contained in twelve plastic filing cabinet-style boxes packed into the Mitsubishi alongside a booster charge made of TNT. The boxes were linked to each other and to the TNT by 150 metres of PETN-filled detonating cord and initiated by ninety-four electric detonators attached to the cord and set off by a battery-powered initiator activated by the driver.

The main bomb was thus way bigger than the Australians' first estimate, but, before I continue, I should perhaps make the situation clear here. The Australian team were the lead agency, we and others were only there to advise and help them, and theirs was the final report. It was a very measured report, and I think they did a fine job. I also think our presence had a very helpful steadying and guiding effect, based on our greater experience of large vehicle bombs, sadly gained over years of IRA activity in the UK.

Nevertheless, a main point of this story is – experience matters. In my opinion, some elements of their team were a little quick to draw conclusions, and having done so

223

were a bit defensive when challenged. None of what follows was part of their final report, but I was interested to see some years later a presentation based on some of their initial conclusions, in particular about the size of the bomb. In that presentation they hadn't abandoned their initial assumption based on the computer's assessment of the crater. Even after the details had emerged, some continued to say it had been a much smaller bomb and argued that, even if over 1,000kg of explosive had been assembled, only 150kg had actually gone off. I regard this as extremely unlikely, for one simple reason among many – that the scene would have been covered in unexploded potassium chlorate, which it was not. My take on this is that you can only gain experience by being openminded when faced with evidence that your initial view of some situation was wide of the mark. Perhaps such an opportunity was lost here.

The details revealed at the trials fitted with what we believed at the FEL, though of course we were not able to know exactly how the Mitsubishi bomb had been configured. Either way it was quite a sophisticated improvised device combining different chemicals and explosives with a wealth of detonating cord and detonators. It was a thorough job and it was going to work, and tragically it *did* work. In my view, it worked to its full potential.

I had seen why people love to travel to Bali for their holidays and I had understood the bewilderment and fury of the locals about what had happened in their midst. They were – to a man and woman – utterly shocked that their island had been picked out for a terrorist attack that destroyed not only the peace and tranquillity for which the area was famous, but seriously damaged the tourist industry upon which so many of them relied for their income. The spectre of terrorism would return to haunt them in 2005, when more suicide bombings in Kuta and at another location in the south of Bali killed another twenty people.

If it had been me alone making the decision, I have no doubt I would have gone back to Bali. As it happened, the following year Vanessa and I were planning a hot holiday to get away from a wet and miserable English winter and we discussed going there but decided it was too far to fly. In truth, I'm not sure Vanessa really fancied the idea of going somewhere where I had so recently been for work. In the end, we booked a place in the Seychelles, where we stayed in a beachside hotel that was similar to the one I had been put up in near Kuta.

As I sat on my sun lounger, Bali did come to mind, but I am pleased to report it was not the bad bits – it was the good bits: the great people and the dignity they showed in such appalling circumstances. I was glad that I could focus on the positive side of it all, and what a lovely place it was and still is.

17

The Shoe Bomber – a transatlantic jigsaw

The irony was not lost on me. I was several weeks into my investigation of a plot to blow up an American airliner in the mid-Atlantic, which could have killed 300 people, and I was travelling with some of the explosive involved – on an airliner across the Atlantic.

As we made our way from Heathrow to San Francisco on a scheduled airline service, I watched the ocean far below me and wondered what my fellow passengers would think if they knew what we had on board.

No doubt some of them would have reacted with understandable trepidation – even shock – and probably would have refused to fly. But most, I guessed, would have taken a rational view once the situation had been explained to them. In truth, the risk to that aircraft was zero.

But being in a plane in those circumstances – taking explosive material that had been intended for use in a shoe bomb to be detonated at 35,000 ft to America for tests – did bring home to me the full horror of what Richard Reid and Saajid Badat had been planning. No one knows for sure what would have happened had a bomb of that kind exploded in mid-air, but the mere thought of a plane hurtling out of control towards the bottom of the ocean was enough to send a shiver down my spine as we continued on our way westwards.

My flight to America in mid-February 2004 came almost three months after I had been scrambled from the Fort to a police incident in Gloucester. In fact, the SO13 liaison officer was so quick off the mark that morning that he organised a police helicopter to pick me up. The word was, the Anti-Terrorist Command had apprehended a young man they believed had been working with Richard Reid.

Reid was the British-born terrorist who had been convicted in a court in Boston in October 2002 of attempting to destroy an airliner using a bomb concealed in the heel of his shoe. Up until that point it had been assumed that Reid was working alone, but the arrest of 24-year-old Saajid Badat changed all that.

This would not be primarily a case about working out whether a bomb had been used, or what explosives it might contain, though the latter was a question we did address. No, this was a case where the key was to try to show that what we found in Britain was the mirror image of bomb components that the FBI had recovered from Reid.

We wanted to demonstrate that they had both received components from the same source, probably an al-Qaeda training camp in Afghanistan or Pakistan. It was like fitting a jigsaw together when the parts were thousands of miles apart and showing that there were chemical and structural similarities in the explosive compounds that were beyond mere coincidences, and then being able to defend that in court.

I grabbed a white forensic suit and some gloves and jumped aboard the chopper for a flight across southern England on a bitterly cold late autumn morning. I knew a bit about the Reid case and had seen the FBI's pictures of his device. I had also viewed a video of a test they had carried out that showed that the explosive in his shoe was powerful enough to blow a hole in the fuselage of a passenger plane, and Lockerbie had drilled into me what the consequences of that were likely to be.

So I was curious to see what had been found in Gloucester. The Reid bomb consisted of a slow-burning safety fuse running into a small package acting as an improvised detonator, from which a detonating cord ran around a lump of plastic explosive. This had all been concealed in the hollowed-out heel of a shoe with only the end of the safety fuse protruding. Reid had been wrestled to the floor, handcuffed and subdued after cabin staff on a flight from Paris to Miami noticed him trying to light the safety fuse using a match with the shoe on his lap.

We landed in a field on the edge of Gloucester, where I was picked up by a waiting police car and then driven at speed to the Badat family home in St James Street in the Barton area of the city. This part of town was popular with the 4,000-strong Muslim population in Gloucester and the house was not far from the mosque where Badat preached. That morning more than 100 families had been evacuated following Badat's arrest, something that had been greeted with astonishment by his neighbours.

Born in Gloucester to a strict Muslim family who had moved to England from Malawi, Badat had been a popular and diligent pupil at his local grammar school, but had been radicalised during a trip to Pakistan and Afghanistan. It was while he was out there that he met Reid, a petty criminal from London who had been introduced to Islamic extremism at a south London mosque.

When I got to the address and made my way through the cordon, there was a bit of banter at my expense among the police officers in attendance. It turned out that the SO13 officer in charge – a chief super – who would normally expect to use the helicopter to travel to a terrorism crime scene from London, had had to come by road. It was pointed out that I'd got there first in *his* chopper.

'No problem with the traffic then, I presume, Cliff,' was how his colleagues greeted me outside the modest two-up, two-down Victorian terraced-house where Badat lived.

After being arrested as a result of intelligence work following a tip-off, Badat was by that time already being questioned at London's high-security Paddington Green police station. He had revealed to officers that he had planned to follow Reid's example in December 2001 and blow up an airliner at the same time as his accomplice, but had changed his mind several days before he was due to carry out his suicide mission on a flight from Amsterdam to the United States.

He had also said that he had since dismantled his bomb and indicated where the various components might be found at the family home. These potentially lethal items – minus the shoe itself, which was later found in his locker at his mosque – had been sitting either in a suitcase or on a shelf in a terraced house in the middle of Gloucester for more than two years.

The army bomb disposal officer had been there for some hours and was waiting for me when I got inside. It was clear that a thorough search had been carried out.

'So what have we got?' I asked him, pulling on my white overalls as we made our way into the back garden, away from prying eyes.

'Well, I've got a section of safety fuse with a taped package on the end that looks like the detonator,' he said. 'Obviously we want to try to preserve as much evidence as possible but I'm not sure exactly what's in this,' he added, pointing to a small white package wrapped in masking tape lying in a metal tray.

We were looking at a 5-inch length of black-plastic-encased cord – the safety fuse that Badat would have set alight using a match or lighter, just as Reid had attempted. It fed into a package that looked as though it consisted of some paper that had been coiled, as if around a biro. Inside that package we knew there was a compound of some kind that was going to be the detonator for the bomb. We both knew this was by far the most dangerous and possibly unstable component of what had been found at the house. Anyone mishandling it could lose a couple of fingers.

But what was it that Badat had used in the package? The most likely candidates were TATP or HMTD, and both would be present in the form of a white powder.

The bomb disposal officer wanted to try out a new testing kit supplied by the army that could identify by means of a colour chart exactly which compound we were dealing with. But it didn't work.

'If it was me,' I told him, 'I'd do a burn test.'

He explained that he had never been trained in that procedure. My view was that I couldn't really care less whether it was TATP or HMTD – I just wanted to know whether Badat had used a dangerous primary explosive or not and a burn test would tell me that.

'OK, so I'll do it,' I replied, digging a cigarette lighter out of my pocket.

We collected a small sample of the damp powder on a spatula and I flicked the lighter into action. As I bought the flame to bear under the spatula there was an immediate orange flash – not a bang – but a bright flash. This was a sure sign that this was indeed primary explosive that was intended to ignite the detonator cord and the plastic explosive in Badat's shoe.

'Thought so . . .' I muttered, as we stood back in silence for a second.

This was going to be critical evidence in any trial involving Badat, so we needed to get it back to the Fort. We packaged it all up with samples of the powder in vials and then placed them inside padded ammunition boxes ready for being transported by road to the lab, where further analysis confirmed it was indeed TATP.

Then the bomb disposal officer showed me the plastic explosive that had been found – an innocuous-looking white lump weighing about 8oz that could have destroyed a 747 and the lives of hundreds of people inside it. Now it was sitting disconnected from the materials that could ignite it on a table in the garden of Badat's home. I had seen this countless times – an explosive material that is mixed with resins, oils and waxes so that it forms a putty that can be moulded into shape. It was the perfect tool for a shoe bomb, where the hollowed-out heel limited the size and shape of any explosive charge.

On its own, plastic explosive – which is used by the military all over the world – is fairly harmless. Squaddies sometimes chop small sections of it off to light fires because it burns steadily, reacting quite differently to the shock blast that occurs when it is connected to a detonator. Not that this is something they are officially supposed to do, and is certainly not recommended, but squaddies are not best known for their blind observance of official rules if it doesn't suit them. And, in truth, surprising though it may seem, with small amounts of commercial plastic explosives, this is not a particularly dangerous thing to do.

I did a burn test on a small sample, which confirmed to me that there was nothing unusual in this sample, though I was still not sure exactly what the main explosive ingredient was. Then we packed that up too alongside the detonator cord that had been found with it.

It was time to go. By then the helicopter was long gone, so I went back to the Fort in a police car with the components we had found at the house – I'm sure not many chopper pilots would have wanted to fly with them on board anyway.

On the way home I mulled over what we had seen: a bomb designed to evade airport security and kill not only its perpetrator but everyone else on board a plane with him; a bomb that had changed airport security procedures for ever.

Mulling over what I knew about Reid, I was already thinking about the real challenge in this case. We were going to want to show that Badat and Reid were rotten apples from the same barrel, as it were. We knew Reid had been trained at camps in Afghanistan and had acquired bomb-making material there. The case against Badat would be overwhelming if we could show that his shoe bomb was supplied from the same source. Could we match the plastic explosive and the detonator cord with what the FBI had?

Over the next few weeks in the run-up to Christmas, we conducted further analysis on the items from the house, measuring, photographing and describing them according to standard procedure. The single explosive ingredient in the plastic explosive turned out to be pentaerythritol tetranitrate or PETN. This powerful explosive belongs to the same chemical family as nitroglycerin and is often present together with another explosive, RDX, in some forms of Semtex plastic explosive. However, it is not commonly the single explosive component of commercial plastic explosives, which this appeared to be, so this was quite an unusual brand, at least in the West.

As our research progressed we opened lines of communication with the FBI and, after discussing it with my opposite number in Boston, where Reid's plane had been diverted, we decided to meet.

Just over two weeks after recovering the materials in Gloucester, I flew with two police officers to Boston. We sat down with our American colleagues and looked at their forensic investigation notes on the shoe bomb they had recovered and pictures of the components, and compared them with the material we had at the Fort. There was no doubt that the similarities were striking, but it was going to take detailed analysis to prove that for court purposes. We decided to go ahead and compare some real samples. That meant going home and flying back with explosive material for analysis in the States.

I am happy to report that it is not easy to fly with explosives in the cargo hold of a transatlantic passenger jet, even if you are the principal forensic investigator with the Ministry of Defence's Forensic Explosive Laboratory. We wanted to take a tiny sample of Badat's plastic explosive and an equally tiny sample of explosive from the detonating cord – which we had also found to be PETN – to be tested by experts at the University of Utah, and going by ship would not have been practical. So we selected a scheduled flight from London Heathrow to San Francisco, where we would change for another flight to Salt Lake City.

The paperwork required was phenomenal even though we were talking about a couple of grams of explosive and no more. I was again accompanied by two police officers, who brought the samples stored in vials in a specially certified cylindrical container that was designed to ensure that, if there was an explosion, it would be completely contained within it.

When we got to Heathrow, the police explained to the pilot why we were taking these substances to America and showed him the container. He informed us that he was happy enough to allow it on board. The cylinder travelled in the cargo hold and was taken off before any other baggage at San Francisco and then transferred, via an airside waiting area, to our connecting flight. The bureaucratic and security palaver around that journey reassured me that the airlines industry was taking no chances after Richard Reid's failed bomb plot.

We were heading to the University of Utah because scientists at its department of biology were leading researchers and practitioners in the relatively new chemical analysis technique known as isotope-ratio mass spectrometry or IRMS. This is a technique that can identify a sample of just about anything by measuring the relative abundance of isotopes in a given substance. Because it is so accurate, it is a brilliant tool to use to show differences and also similarities between two samples of the same material – for example, human hair or skin, the contents of someone's stomach or explosives.

In our case we knew we had conventional plastic explosive and detonator cord explosive, but we needed to see if they were identical to the equivalent components in Reid's bomb. The important thing was to make a comparison under controlled conditions to ensure that no defence barrister could pick apart what we had done and say, for example, that irregularities in the testing procedure made the findings unreliable.

We knew quite a lot about IRMS at the FEL because we had been looking at its introduction into our analysis programme, but we had not yet incorporated it into our lab practice. The scientists at the University of Utah were leading the field in its use with explosives, so this was clearly the best place to carry out the analysis under the expert guidance of Dr James Ehleringer.

My job was to watch what Ehleringer was doing in a supervisory role. This fulfilled a court convention that allows an expert witness – in my case a forensic scientist – to present a case based on experimental analysis even though they may not have carried out the detailed experiment themselves. My role, alongside colleagues from the FBI, was to watch and monitor what was happening.

The key to IRMS is measuring the ratio of so-called heavy to light isotopes in an element. PETN contains the elements carbon, hydrogen, oxygen and nitrogen and we chose carbon and nitrogen for our isotope-ratio analysis. The principle behind it is that the isotope-ratio of a particular material can change as a result of chemical, physical or biological processes that it may be subject to. Thus, for instance, when PETN is manufactured, the isotope ratios of its elements will depend on many factors like the starting ingredients and the exact chemical processes and conditions used to produce it. IRMS is a clever way of working out whether materials are more or less identical or divergent in some way.

The analysis that Dr Ehleringer and his team carried out was not a simple or rapid process, and took two days to complete. The IRMS machine was perhaps the size of a small desk, and is an extremely complex and sophisticated piece of equipment. Although each individual sample might take only a few minutes to run when put into the machine, they all first needed to be chemically treated to render them into the right form to be presented to it.

As IRMS is an extremely delicate and sensitive measuring tool, it needed to be calibrated with known standards, both before and during the analysis of the samples. And many control samples, which verified the validity of the samples in question, had to be prepared and run alongside them. These needed to be run more than once, initially just the British ones by themselves, and then again alongside the FBI samples. All this, as mentioned, took two days to complete, so while I stayed to observe in the lab, the rest of the team took advantage of the downtime – and went skiing.

The upshot of all this work was that it clearly demonstrated that the PETN from the detonating cord samples held by us and the FBI showed values for carbon and nitrogen that lay in the same statistical range. We reached the same conclusion about the PETN from the plastic-explosive samples that Reid and Badat had used. We had no doubt that the samples in each case matched but it was now my job to interpret our findings. IRMS analysis of explosive had never been presented as evidence in a British court before and I was nervous about being caught out by an astute barrister, perhaps relying on an expert statistician.

The crux of my argument was to demonstrate that the similarities we had detected stood up against previous background data on plastic explosive and that our samples remained closer to each other in form than any other samples previously tested. In the end, I was confident that I could argue that the chemical formulation of the plastic explosive we had found at St James Street was very similar to the explosive in the hands of the FBI, consistent with them having originated from the same proprietary brand. And, indeed, very likely from the same batch of that brand.

As the trial approached in February 2005, I was feeling confident and even looking forward to appearing in the witness box. Our view at the Fort was that although there was a risk my evidence could be subjected to potentially damaging scrutiny, we felt that would not be critical to the outcome of the overall case against Badat, which relied on a lot of other solid evidence. We also felt that this was an ideal opportunity to learn about using IRMS testing in court and see how it fared under pressure of cross-examination.

In the end all our preparation work came to nought when Badat, realising he was looking at thirty years if he was convicted, decided to plead guilty at the last minute. A couple of months later he was jailed for thirteen years, a sentence that was cut by two years after he struck a secret deal to turn supergrass against al-Qaeda, another first in this case.

I wouldn't say that Badat and Reid's devices were crude – I think they had a fair chance of success. It is humanity's good fortune that they never achieved the aims for which they were intended. We can never say never, but it looks unlikely that that avenue – a shoe bomb – could now be used by a terrorist to bring down an airliner, with airport security scanning and X-ray imaging steadily improving.

However, I have wondered whether we could have worked out what Reid had done if his bomb had detonated. Had the Paris to Miami flight come down over the ocean, we would probably never have known what had happened. But over land I feel confident it would have been a different story and we would have had a fair chance of tracing it back to even a small amount of explosive in a shoe.

Obviously the scene of the crash would have to be properly protected and its debris fully recovered, but then there would be a reasonable chance that, just as we did at Lockerbie, we would have discovered tiny fragments of shoe embedded in bits of the aluminium fuselage and in fragments of insulation. It might well have been enough to set us working on the theory that a bomb had been concealed on the plane in someone's shoe, even if we might not be able to say precisely how it was formed or set off.

18

Exploding limousines . . . on paper . . .

The case that became known as the 'Gas Limos Project' intrigued me from the start. It was not just that it was all on paper – unlike all the other cases in this book, no bombs or devices were actually built – but also the challenge of trying to show that someone's intention to do something was credible and could actually happen in the real world.

Anybody can go on to the internet or visit public libraries to research how to build bombs, and even sketch out plans to attack specific targets. But at what point does that planning cross over from being a possibly unattainable ambition to something potentially real and dangerous? If a bomber starts to buy components, then he, or she, is likely to be bang to rights before the law; but if he, or she, does not get to that stage, then it is all about *intention* – is the plan likely to happen and, if so, will it work?

In this instance the plan hatched by the Hindu-born al-Qaeda terrorist Dhiren Barot amounted to one of the most terrifyingly destructive schemes I came across at the FEL, and one that could have killed hundreds, if not thousands, of people in simultaneous attacks on both sides of the Atlantic.

Barot's bombing ideas were imaginative, unusual and ambitious. They included detonating a 'dirty bomb' that would spread radioactive contamination in either London or New York; an attack on the Heathrow Express train service that links the airport with Paddington station; an attempt to blow up and flood the London Underground network with a bomb in a tunnel under the Thames; and plans to hijack petrol tankers and ram them into pre-selected targets.

The part of it that I was concerned with was his scheme to try to bring down a major building, possibly in New York or Washington. He aimed to achieve this by detonating an improvised and quite complex bomb delivered in three stretch limos packed full of propane or butane gas bottles to a basement underground car park.

Barot's plan could have caused a series of huge explosions or possibly a fuel-air explosion under a skyscraper. Having studied it, I became convinced that this was a credible proposition, even if Barot did not fully understand the chemistry of what he was attempting, and I was looking forward to explaining why in a court of law. But, to my surprise – and, to be frank, disappointment – Barot decided to plead guilty and I never got my chance.

This case started in July 2004, when security forces in Pakistan raided an al-Qaeda cell and seized a laptop on which they found a thirty-nine-page document entitled 'The Gas Limos Project' that they were able to link to Barot as its author. He was a British citizen who was subsequently detained near London the following month.

The case was regarded as highly sensitive from a national security point of view, and was shrouded in secrecy and court orders restricting reporting of it from the start. And when the document arrived at the FEL from the Met's SO13 anti-terrorist branch and MI5, there were still concerns – later resolved – over whether the way it had been obtained would make it admissible in a British court.

When it reached the FEL, I had been running the case-work department for more than six years and had long since stopped taking on individual investigations, busy as I was overseeing the work of everyone reporting to me. But this conspiracy hatched by Barot caught my eye. Not only did it involve a possible fuel-air explosion – an area that I was probably the most experienced in, having worked on the IRA's Warrington gasworks bombing a decade earlier – but also because it was a 'documents only' case, albeit a huge one. It turned out that Barot had accumulated a library of information and research stretching to more than 5,000 pages on his computer, all of which would have to be gone through as part of the evaluation of the 'Gas Limos' file.

In my position, a documents case particularly appealed to me because it did not involve lab work. I had always thoroughly enjoyed casework, but as my management responsibilities grew, I had gradually stopped working in the lab and begun to lose my proficiency in many of the techniques that lie at the heart of forensic explosives research. Back in the early 2000s, the FEL was starting to come under new and stringent measures to ensure that all casework officers were up to scratch on lab techniques – for example, the methods and practice of explosives trace analysis – with regular proficiency tests by outside inspectors and I knew I would struggle to pass some of them. But a documents case was something I could still get my teeth into and I got to work.

Aged thirty-four at the time of his arrest, Barot was an introspective character who had been born in India into a respectable middle-class family from Vadodara in Gujarat. When he was one, the family emigrated to Kenya, but, after suffering violence and discrimination there, they left after a year and moved to England. His father, who had been a banker in India, had to make do with a job in a factory in northeast London.

Barot was raised in the Hindu religion and went to school locally in the Kingsbury area of London. To start with his life looked unremarkable enough. After leaving school in 1988, he obtained a City and Guilds qualification in tourism, studied hotel management and then worked for four years as an airline ticketing clerk in Piccadilly in central London. On leaving that role he took up a series of odd jobs, working as a night porter in a block of flats and for a mobile phone company.

At some point his interest in Islamic extremism developed and, in the summer of 1995, he told his employers he was going away on a 'long overseas trip'. In fact he travelled to Pakistan, where he visited terrorist training camps on the Pakistan–Afghanistan border and took part in fighting in the long-running Indo-Pakistan dispute over Pakistan-occupied Kashmir. In 1999, by which time he had converted to Islam, he authored a book under the name Abu Esa Al Hindi about his experiences in Pakistan, entitled *The Army of Madinah in Kashmir*, in which he described ways to kill Indian soldiers.

Barot had come into contact with al-Qaeda terrorists in Pakistan, including one of the masterminds of the 9/11 attacks, Khalid Sheikh Mohammad, and, in 2000 and 2001, he made trips to the United States on their behalf, on the pretext of studying at university. But after reviewing footage he had taken on video, which had been seized in a raid on a London lock-up garage, MI5 and SO13 officers believed these were surveillance exercises for possible attacks on US cities. Among the buildings Barot is thought to have checked out were the headquarters of the World Bank and International Monetary Fund in Washington and the Stock Exchange and Citigroup buildings in New York.

The thirty-nine-page 'Gas Limos' file was written as if requesting permission – presumably from his al-Qaeda masters – for approval to proceed with a series of attacks, not least the attempt to bring one of these major buildings to the ground.

Barot's plan envisaged getting hold of three stretch limos or other suitable vehicles that might not attract undue attention in downtown New York or Washington. These would be filled with large butane or propane cylinders and several cans of nails as shrapnel and driven into an underground car park.

The defence argued in court prior to his sentencing that not only did Barot not have the funds to make any of this happen, but that far from being an al-Qaeda mastermind he was a hapless plotter who really did not have a clue about what he was attempting. When I first read his document, I kept an open mind about this. Just how serious was he? Did he know what he was talking about? Could his plan work? It did not take me long to realise that this was indeed a serious prospectus for a major terrorist attack that had been exhaustively researched and that it could work.

Perhaps the most important issue was whether Barot knew enough about what he was doing to be a credible bomber. I could tell that he was not a trained chemist because of the way he confused various potential outcomes, but he demonstrated enough of a grasp of key fundamentals for this not to matter. He understood for example that, for this multi-faceted improvised device to have a chance of detonating at full scale – which could be a fuel-air explosion – it needed to be set up in a confined area such as an underground car park.

He understood too that at least some of cylinders would need to be opened to enable gas to escape and then mix with oxygen in the air to create an explosive combination. This could be achieved by the movement of people and cars in the car park and the influences on the air of mechanical ventilation and air purification systems. Most critically of all, his writing demonstrated that he understood there was a time element with the mixing to consider that few people properly understood, but Barot had grasped it.

He was aiming, in this context, for something that the military have been trying to achieve for decades, a fuel-air explosion on command that unleashes enormous forces over a wide area and, in this case, would be capable of destroying the main foundation pillars of a modern sky-scraper.

Barot's writing also made clear that he grasped less-dramatic outcomes, not least what is known as a BLEVE, or boiling-liquid expanding-vapour explosion. This occurs when a vented high-pressure cylinder filled with propane or butane is heated from the outside to the point where the gas inside begins to boil and ultimately explodes in a violent incendiary event. The outcome of Barot's planning may not have been a full-scale fuel-air explosion, but it may well have been a series of BLEVE events, as one cylinder after another exploded, creating a massive fireball in the car park.

I could not be sure which of these two outcomes was uppermost in Barot's mind. But I was certain that his plans would lead to something dangerously destructive. In my statement to Woolwich Crown Court, which was never used in open proceedings but would have been read by the judge, Mr Justice Butterfield, I set out a range of possible outcomes that could happen but without committing myself to any one of them as a certainty.

At the least destructive end of the spectrum would be a fire that could be doused by prompt action from an effective sprinkler system. The next possibility was a much larger fire that could seriously threaten a building and those in it, then a series of BLEVE explosions sending burning material shooting into the air, and finally a large vapour cloud explosion causing the complete destruction of the target building.

I knew that, if the case had gone to trial, I would have faced detailed questioning about the behaviour of a vapour cloud and how easy or not it would be to achieve the right gas–air mix and then successfully detonate it. This was ground that I had been quizzed on during the Warrington case and I felt confident that I could deal with a hostile cross-examination on this area.

There were also gaps in Barot's account that he could use to his advantage, not least the absence of a description of a timing device. However, in and amongst the thousands of pages of research carried out by him, there was lots of good information that could have been brought to bear about how to make and deploy improvised timers.

Looking back, it is interesting to reflect on the fact that this case occurred in the years immediately after 9/11, when the full ambition of al-Qaeda's terrorist activities were still very much in the forefront of all our minds. However, I do not believe that our knowledge of what had happened in Manhattan in September 2001 influenced my view of Barot's intent or what was possible.

The judge told Barot that his plan for multiple back-to-back attacks, including the limousine one, was designed to strike at the 'very heart of democracy and the security of the state'. He described Barot's approach as 'business-like', which very much reflected my own impressions of his writing – and that it showed a seriousness of purpose that made it credible. He said that if Barot's plot had come to fruition it would have affected 'thousands personally, millions indirectly, and ultimately the whole nations of the US and UK'.

Peter Clarke, the head of SO13, described Barot as a 'full-time terrorist' who had used anti-surveillance techniques, coded messages and secret meetings to try to evade capture. He said his conviction was a landmark in the fight against terrorism in the United Kingdom. 'For well over two years we have been unable to show the British public the reality of the threat they faced from this man,' he said. 'Now they can see for themselves the full horror of his plans.'

I never imagined Barot would plead guilty. Almost all terrorist offenders, whether they be from the ranks of the IRA or Islamic extremists, fight to the last, occupying the legal system with trials and appeals and using the legal process, and the reporting of it in the press, to help promote their ideals. Barot would have had a strong case to argue centred on the whole question of intent and I would have been a key expert witness for the prosecution.

In the event, in November 2007, he was handed an exceptionally long sentence of forty years before consideration could be given to parole. Six months later that sentence was cut to thirty years by three Court of Appeal judges, who noted that expert scientific evidence had shown that, as they put it, the 'exploding limousines' project was superficially attractive although 'amateurish'.

The idea of using gas canisters in vehicles as bombs was revisited by Islamic extremist terrorists in Britain a month after Barot's appeal, when two car bombs were deployed in London and then another at Glasgow airport. The bombs in London failed to detonate due to a minor design fault, demonstrating the difficulty of using gas bottles to create an explosion.

The car in Glasgow – a Cherokee Jeep occupied by two men and loaded with several petrol containers and propane canisters – was rammed into the doors of Glasgow airport terminal building. The jeep failed to ignite, prompting one of the men to start throwing petrol bombs from the passenger seat while his accomplice got out, doused himself in petrol and set himself on fire. He died later in hospital. Several other people were injured helping police detain the pair.

It had been a fairly ham-fisted effort to achieve a BLEVE event using propane in a vehicle, but its failure never prompted me to seriously review whether Barot would have fared any better. His plan was much more comprehensive and better thought out.

19

7/7 – feeling the pressure when the country is waiting for answers

I had been in the tunnel on the westbound Circle Line between King's Cross and Russell Square on London's Underground for nearly two hours viewing the handiwork of the nineteen-year-old suicide bomber Germaine Lindsay.

He had detonated his device during the early morning rush hour on 7 July 2005, killing twenty-six people on the train as it made its way along the Piccadilly line, southbound from King's Cross towards Russell Square.

Elsewhere on the Underground two other suicide bombers had detonated their charges at Edgware Road, where six people were killed, and at Aldgate, where another seven died.

Then, shortly afterwards, a fourth member of the gang, who had travelled down to London early that morning from Leeds via Luton to carry out their al-Qaeda-inspired attack, detonated a bomb on the upper deck of a London bus at Tavistock Square, not far from King's Cross. That explosion killed thirteen more people.

7/7 – feeling the pressure

The death toll in what was the single deadliest terror-ist outrage in modern English history and Britain's first Islamist suicide bombing was fifty-six, including the four bombers, with another 784 people injured.

The atmosphere in central London on a day that will for ever be remembered as '7/7' was fraught with fear, tension and anger as the general public came to terms with what had happened in their midst.

The pressure on the government – and on the police and the security services – to establish who had done this, how they had carried out their attack, and whether further similar attacks were likely was enormous. I remember feel-ing it like a physical weight on all our shoulders as I and my teams from the FEL made our way to the various scenes to help in that effort.

'Okay, Cliff, now you've seen it – what can you tell us?'

It was the insistent voice of the detective in charge of the police operation at Russell Square and he was waiting impatiently for my opinion on what I had seen, which was about as close to a vision of hell as I am ever likely to come across.

Down in that dark tunnel, all the living and injured had been evacuated but the dead remained in a gross still life, created by the forms of their bodies and body parts, while forensic work continued in what was now an investigation into a mass murder.

EXPLOSIVE

People often say to me that I must have witnessed some terrible things in my time at the FEL, but the truth of the matter is that I would generally arrive at the scenes of bomb attacks many hours, or even days, after an explosion and by which time the dead had almost always already been recovered. I did see bodies at various places, and I had a good idea of what a corpse that had been close to a high-explosive detonation could look like, but Russell Square was still a huge shock to my system.

As I toured the broken carriages of that train, stepping gingerly between the bodies on floors that were slippery with blood and gore, I could feel the almost tangible threat of being overwhelmed by the sheer brutality of what I was looking at. For the last twenty years of my professional life I had worked on trying to understand improvised explosives and bombs – pipe bombs, booby traps, car bombs, shoe bombs, lorry bombs – but never had I been confronted with such a visceral and stomach-churning tableau of what those things could do to the human body.

My defence against emotional overload was to almost physically push back against it. It was a conscious thought in the darkness. 'You can't let this get to you, Cliff, so concentrate,' I told myself. 'Concentrate on what you need to do and ignore what you're actually seeing. Don't think about it, don't think about who these people were or what the survivors must have seen before they were evacuated, just focus on what you need to do to help the police.'

7/7 – feeling the pressure

In reply to the detective, I was tempted to resort to black humour and say something flippant along the lines of 'Well, it looks a like a bomb might have gone off down there.'

But after giving myself a moment to focus, with the help of a couple of deep breaths of fresh air, I gave the officer my best opinion.

'Okay,' I said, 'I'd say several kilograms of high explosive detonated, at or close to floor level, in the standing area beside the second set of doors from the front of the first carriage of the train.'

So far so good and so uncontroversial. I knew this didn't deal with the main question the police were desperate to get an answer to – was this the work of a suicide bomber? Or had someone left a device on the train and could that person still be out there ready to strike again?

I could feel the pressure building on a day when initial speculation had suggested a power surge had caused the various explosions on the Underground network. We had all travelled a long way in a short time since those early reports and now the police wanted me to go one step further than I was happy to do without more time to examine the scene.

So, with my fingers and all other available appendages firmly crossed, I ventured further into some educated guesswork.

'As regards how this was delivered, I can't say for sure, but my guess is this was the work of a suicide attacker,' I told him.

Then I quickly added all the usual forensic science caveats about the need for more time at the scene and further gathering of samples. I also reminded him that bodies had been moved around during the rescue operation, so their positions could no longer be used to work out the exact sequence of events. I knew full well that all this would be politely received – as it was – and just as swiftly forgotten.

Although I'd stuck my neck out at a moment when people in charge of what would become one of the biggest anti-terrorist investigations in English history wanted answers, my view was not entirely unfounded. I hadn't examined, or even properly seen, all the bodies in the tunnel about 100 ft below where we were standing, but one had stood out to me.

Most of the victims had severe trauma, and traumatic amputations to their lower limbs and trunk, but facially they had been largely intact. That was the case with all that I had seen except for one, who seemed to have suffered more damage to the trunk and who had almost no face remaining. With a device placed at floor level, and not being carried at chest or back height, I could see this kind of damage being caused if someone was crouching down next to it, perhaps to trigger it.

7/7 – feeling the pressure

As the investigation developed, the first question on our minds at the FEL was what sort of explosive had been used at each of the four locations. This was something we would normally expect to clear up within hours or, at most, a few days of an incident of this scale and importance. But this time – when the eyes of the world were focused on London – it would be different, and frustratingly so.

At Russell Square my colleagues and I had spent time taking extensive swab samples in a setting where that was not the easiest of tasks to complete. Human remains and body fluids had been projected over almost all the available surfaces close to the seat of the detonation and we knew they tended to degrade explosives residue. The upshot was we had to find areas that looked clean and similar approaches were taken by our colleagues at the other bomb sites on the Underground.

We got the samples back to the FEL and began work, testing them for all the explosive compounds that we were familiar with – RDX, PETN, TNT, nitroglycerine and then inorganic explosives like the IRA had used – ammonium-nitrate-based mixtures, and then gunpowder and pyro-technic materials. The result was a total blank. We simply had no idea what had been used at any of the four sites in London.

As the person in charge of the casework section of the FEL, I felt frustrated and puzzled and I could feel the heat because everyone from the Home Secretary down wanted an answer we could not provide.

Two days after the attacks I received the latest in a series of calls from senior officers at the Metropolitan police.

'Morning, Cliff, so have you got what we need to know?'

'No, and yeah, good morning, Nick.'

'Well, why not?'

'Because the tests we have done so far are coming up negative and we cannot just make it up, can we?'

'But you guys investigated the IRA for years and everything else that has ever happened since, so why the hell can't you understand what this is, for chrissake?'

'Well, perhaps because this is not the IRA . . .'

I knew this guy pretty well and we were on friendly terms, but I could tell he was getting exasperated.

'How long d'you think it's going to take?'

'I dunno. It's going to take as long as it takes,' I replied unhelpfully. 'We are working on it, Nick, as we speak, and we will not stop until we find the answer we are looking for. In the meantime, I suggest you take a chill pill . . .'

That may not have been the most diplomatic advice in the circumstances. There was a long silence before he bade me farewell with an irritable 'good luck' and the call ended.

I put the phone down on my desk and rubbed my head in my hands. I knew we had to sort this out and fast. It seemed the cruellest of ill-fortune that the bomb-makers in the biggest mass murder in Britain since Lockerbie, nearly twenty years earlier, had managed to come up with a con-coction we had never seen before and that we had no test for. At the FEL we didn't always come up with findings after three or four days, but it was rare to draw a complete blank with no pointers or hints of where we should be looking in that time.

Luckily for us and everyone else involved with this investigation, the police made two major breakthroughs on the fifth day after the attacks. They discovered two cars used by the bombers that had been left at Luton station and a series of addresses used by them in the Leeds–Bradford area, including a two-bedroomed ground-floor flat that appeared to be a bomb factory.

This changed everything. No longer would we be having to deal with only trace samples; now we had a chance of getting hold of the explosive materials themselves, which would allow us to start piecing together what this gang had been up to. I felt more relieved than anything, because now we would have answers to the key questions . . . or so I thought.

While two of my staff were despatched to Leeds by helicopter – everything was done in a rush and at fever pitch – I got on the phone to the police EXPO at Luton and talked through with him what he had found. The cars had been cordoned off after police had identified the gang on the platform at Luton on CCTV footage on the morning of the attacks.

EXPLOSIVE

One of the cars, a Nissan Micra, had a bag in the boot with around twelve devices in it. These consisted of clear glass Petri dishes with a white powder inside them, some with nails stuck to their outside surfaces. The lids were held down by Parafilm – a heavy-duty version of Clingfilm. There was no detonator with any of them and it looked as though these had been built as improvised hand grenades, presumably to target police officers or even the general public. Assuming the white powder was a form of unstable high explosive, these would simply have to be thrown and would explode on impact.

The EXPO had removed the bag and placed the devices on a tarpaulin on the ground.

'I think the best thing for me to do is to zap them with the robot,' he told me.

I knew that this would probably mean we would lose vital evidence in the investigation.

'Look, if you do that, is there any way you could cover them with sandbags so that we could recover all the debris for trace testing?' I asked him.

It was never our policy at the FEL to advise an EXPO or EOD technician on how to deal with explosives. They had their own protocols to work to and their own safety to consider, but I did feel on this occasion that I could make a request. I was anxious to try to get hold of some of the white powder, thinking it could well be the same substance the bombers had used to detonate their suicide devices.

'We are quite happy with whatever course of action you decide to take and if you destroy them all that's fine with us,' I said. 'But if you think it's feasible to get a sample, that would be a big step forward for us. There's no pressure whatsoever on this; you have to do what you think is the safest thing,' I told him.

However, the EXPO was up for the challenge and said he was willing to have a go. We discussed how a small sample of the powder could be collected and then packed up in a small vial containing a mixture of alcohol and water as a dampener.

I left it with him. He destroyed most of the Petri dishes but, to his considerable credit, he manually opened one, using a scalpel to cut the film holding the lid down, and then removed a small scoop of powder, which he duly packed up as we had discussed. It was a dangerous procedure and I was grateful to him for going beyond the call of duty.

When we got it back to the lab we confirmed within a few hours that this was HMTD. Finally we were starting to make progress on the 7/7 bombers.

The bomb factory at the flat in Leeds was a treasure trove from an evidential point of view, but the story of how we got in there is a sorry tale of delays caused by inexperience and bureaucracy. It turned out that the EOD technician sent to the scene on Alexandra Grove was one of the more inexperienced in the regiment and he was not prepared for what he found in the chaotic ground-floor flat, which was a complete and utter mess.

This was the place where four young men had built the bombs that would end their own lives and those of so many others. As he made his way in, he could barely find clear spaces on the floor to place his feet. It was littered with rubbish of all kinds – food, papers, plastic bags, bottles, tubs of smelly glutinous mixtures of various kinds that the EOD could not identify, filter papers, glass containers with powders in them, face masks, dust masks and gas masks.

The poor guy was used to making bombs safe, not trying to work out what was dangerous and what was not in a heap of rubbish, and he emerged to tell my two colleagues that there was no way they could be allowed in until it was safe to do so.

They managed to persuade him to bring out some samples – and he duly emerged for a second time with a sample of some sludge from one bucket and some white powder from a glass jar, but that was going to be about it for the next five days.

In retrospect this seems almost incredible. There we were trying to investigate as fast possible the biggest terrorist attack on English soil and a young EOD had effectively stopped us in our tracks because, through no fault of his own, he didn't understand what he had been looking at.

While we waited, we got the samples back to the Fort thanks to the RAF's search-and-rescue helicopter based at

Lossiemouth in Scotland that was tasked – in the absence of any other available aircraft – to fly them down to Biggin Hill. The powder turned out to be more HMTD, as we suspected after our discoveries at Luton. But the sludge was a mystery. By the time we started working on it, it was mostly water with some brown matter partially dissolved in it.

I remember looking at it and thinking: 'What the f*** is this?' I had never seen anything like it.

The word from Leeds was that it was possibly a tub of faeces and it certainly looked as though that could be the case. But after a few days of tests we finally discovered that the brown or yellowish matter in the water contained something called piperine, an alkaloid that is responsible for the pungency of peppercorns that you might have sitting on your kitchen table. This did not immediately feel like a breakthrough – we had no prior experience of an explosive mixture involving pepper – and we were still scratching our heads more than a week after the bombings.

The lack of progress in Leeds had become ridiculous and it was irritating senior officers at New Scotland Yard. They called a crisis meeting to deal with it, to which I was invited. I was asked to bring an overnight bag. Because the young EOD had spotted gas masks in the flat, he had become concerned that the gang may have been working on a chemical device of some kind, so experts from the chemical-weapons establishment at Porton Down had been summoned to have a look. They spent a couple of days up there but came to the conclusion that whatever the sludge was, it was not a chemical agent, and packed up and went home.

We sat around a table – senior police officers, people from Porton and others – and we were asked what we thought should happen next. When it was my turn I made it clear that it was long past the time when we should have got into the flat.

'Our colleagues from Porton have said they can't find chemical agents in there, and I am happy with that,' I said. 'There was also no sign of chemical residues at any of the bomb scenes. I am more than prepared to go in with an *experienced* EOD on that basis, because we need to make progress.'

The senior officer was delighted to hear what I had to say and told me, there and then, to get up to Leeds myself and get on with it. There was a police driver waiting for me and, with the blue lights turned on, I was soon on my way up the M1 to al-Qaeda's 7/7 bomb factory.

This time the EOD regiment had sent one of their most experienced operators, who was near the end of his career and he was reassuringly up for the job. He told me he would go in first and have a quick look around and then come back out to get me. I suited up in my white overalls, neoprene gloves and protective goggles and stood sweating in the heat of another scorchingly hot July afternoon.

Twenty minutes later he reappeared and beckoned me forward.

'Okay, I'm happy, let's go, Cliff,' he said, 'just be careful where you put your feet.'

We went in together, talking through everything we saw as we came across it.

Now I had seen a few bomb factories in my time and they were usually pretty messy and disorganised places, but this one was off the charts. The adjective that came to mind, as I wandered round this al-Qaeda laboratory, was 'shithole', and that was no exaggeration. The place was full of rubbish and detritus of all kinds, some of which looked potentially dangerous. It had clearly not been lived in and there was no order to it whatsoever – even the bath was full of half-dissolved brown sludge that looked and apparently smelt like human faeces. Once again, my absence of a sense of smell came in handy.

We made our way around, selecting items for packaging up and sending back to the Fort. As we did so, I noticed a couple of large bags of ground pepper but did not immediately clock their significance. At one point I was examining some tubs of what we came to refer to as 'gloop' when something odd struck me about them. Although the original EOD and the staff at the lab who had tested the samples said they smelled of faeces, I noticed that there wasn't a single fly anywhere near them, even though this was a roaring hot summer's day.

265

EXPLOSIVE

It was then that I began to put it all together – the piperine, the bags of ground pepper and the sludge in the buckets. Clearly they were making bombs using pepper. But what had they mixed it with? There were fluids in the flat in various containers, and hotplates where it looked as though a corrosive substance had been heated. Selecting a sample from one container, I poured some into an empty jar and took it outside, where I dripped a little of it on to a flowerbed. I noticed the soil started fizzing. That certainly caught my eye.

Thinking it could be an acid solution, I tested it with litmus paper, but it came out neutral, so it wasn't alkaline either. It was at that moment that I first considered bleach or hydrogen peroxide that is used in everyday life as hair dye. So maybe that was it? Had the 7/7 bombers used hydrogen peroxide as an oxidiser and pepper as the fuel? In the right proportions they must have found a way to get that combination to act as an explosive, triggered by detonators using HMTD. They must have been using the hotplates to boil the hydrogen peroxide down by reducing its water content to achieve a higher level of concentration than in the products they had bought off the shelves.

Now we really had something to get our teeth into after days of meandering and frustration. I spent two days in Leeds, going through the flat and working with the EOD through all the material that needed to be made safe so that the local residents – who had been evacuated from their homes for nearly a week – could move back in. We sent lots of samples back to the FEL and to other forensic agencies and then started collecting all the rest of the stuff to destroy it there and then.

In order to do this the EOD built a little igloo in the courtyard outside the flat. It was made of sandbags and had a small opening at its base where we could push stuff inside where it would be burnt using an electrical igniter at the end of a long wire. All the while, we were conscious of the fact that the hot summer weather was making everything dry and dusty. Much of the material had powder residues on it and I knew that most of that powder was HMTD and that required delicate handling at the best of times. To be on the safe side, we constantly soaked all the filter papers and other items that we wanted to burn with a 'killer solution' made of an alcohol and water mix.

It was during this process that I experienced one of the very few occasions during my entire career in forensic explosives science when I suddenly had to stop myself as the realisation dawned on me that I was doing something highly dangerous and, in this case, stupid. In fact I heard myself muttering something along the lines of: 'Hey, Cliff, what the f*** do you think you are doing?'

I was on all fours with my head inside the igloo, moving stuff around to make space to accommodate the last lot of material for burning when I looked up. To my horror I saw thousands of motes of dust dancing in the air all around me, lit by the sunlight that was pouring in from behind. It was then that I realised that, far from being safe and damp, the material must have dried out and released particles of HMTD into the igloo all around my face and head. It dawned on me that any sudden movement, or perhaps a sneeze, could be enough to cause an explosion that would have disfigured me or perhaps even killed me.

I stopped what I was doing and very slowly and gingerly began reversing out of the igloo. I emerged no doubt looking somewhat sheepish to be greeted by the EOD with a wry smile on his face. We laughed about it as he moved forward to replace the last sandbags, where my head had been, ready for firing. Both of us knew I had made a silly mistake. It was a reminder that you can never be too careful, and failing to do something as simple as spraying material adequately could be enough to cost you your life in this line of work.

We had more or less finished our duties in Leeds, though the police would spend several more weeks at Alexandra Grove. A group of us were sitting in the little white tent we had put up outside the flat having a chat and a cup of tea when we heard something on the radio that stopped us in our tracks.

The news was led by an item describing 'incidents' at three London Underground stations and on one London bus. Reports were sketchy, there were no details of casualties as yet and further updates would be broadcast as soon as they were available.

It was 21 July 2005 and it felt like déjà-vu. 'Here we go again,' I muttered to myself.

The EOD stood up and chucked his tea on to the grass. 'Right, that's it, then,' he said. 'The gloves have got to come off now . . .'

20

21/7 – detonators but no bombs

I was in Leeds but I needed to be back in London and fast. My phone went red hot. It felt like Britain was under attack and the pace of our investigation, which had started to ease a little in the days after 7/7, suddenly ramped up again.

It was weird – an almost identical pattern of attacks in London – three Tube trains and a bus, but this time there seemed to be no casualties as reports started coming in of small explosions at each scene, leaving the main charge in a rucksack apparently undetonated.

As I headed back down the M1, driven by an officer from the Met's anti-terrorist branch, I was on the phone almost the entire time, speaking to senior police officers and my own staff, who were on their way to the various scenes – at Shepherd's Bush, Warren Street and Oval Underground stations and a No. 26 bus in Bethnal Green.

We could all see that these latest attackers were copying the 7/7 ones, but, unlike them, these terrorists were still alive, and could strike again, so the police were under huge pressure to find them and show that they were on top of this crisis. It was already being billed as Scotland Yard's biggest ever manhunt, driven by CCTV images of the bombers in the lead-up to the attacks.

One aspect of this that none of us were aware of at the time was why both sets of bombers had chosen three Tube trains and one bus. It would later emerge that Hasib Hussain, the eighteen-year-old bus bomber on 7/7, had initially gone into the Underground at King's Cross and may have tried to detonate his bomb, but it did not work.

He was then caught on CCTV buying batteries in WHSmith's at King's Cross and afterwards entering a McDonald's, where he fitted new batteries to his initiator. It was after that that he selected a bus in Tavistock Square. By then it was full of commuters who had been moved off the Underground network because of the bombings else-where, and he detonated his device on the top deck.

Fourteen days later, the 21/7 bombers had slavishly fol-lowed the same pattern even though there was no evidence that their bus bomber – one Mukta Said Ibrahim – had experienced the same difficulties as Hussain.

The frenetic pace of events that day would prove a foretaste of what was to come for me, as the FEL went into overdrive in response to both the 7/7 and 21/7 attacks, requiring us to deal with hundreds of pieces of evidence and multiple concurrent investigations. For me it would mean long days, getting into work at 7.30 or even earlier and staying into the evening in a pattern that became the norm for the next four months. At one point we even instituted a double shift rota at the FEL so that we could continue working in the evenings, something that in the rules and routine-governed world of the civil service was almost unprecedented.

21/7 itself was going to be one of our longest days as we grappled with the highly dangerous mess left by the bombers at each of the four scenes. By that stage we were pretty confident we knew the 7/7 bombers had used a mixture of concentrated hydrogen peroxide and crushed black pepper in their main charges with an HMTD-filled detonator, but the yellowish 'gloop' spilling out of the rucksacks on 21/7 did not look exactly the same as the 7/7 stuff. We had to assume it was a different mix and not rush to any conclusions that could prove fatally incorrect.

We confirmed the early speculation that the popping noises that members of the public had heard at each scene were the sounds of detonators igniting, leaving the main charges untouched while the bombers ran for it. It was a systematic failure on the bombers' part in the way they had built their devices that must have saved so many lives that day.

As the afternoon merged into the evening, I was involved in intensive discussions with the FEL case officers at the scenes and EXPO technicians about how we should go about tackling the mixture that was oozing out of the rucksacks.

By 9.30pm we had come up with a plan. With assistance from the FEL staff at each location, the EXPO would carefully – and little by little – scoop the mix into large, anti-static nylon bags, which would then be taped up and placed inside strong plastic boxes ready for transportation back to the FEL for analysis. Once we had agreed this, I rang around the various scenes and gave the green light; we were underway.

But after an hour or so it became clear that Plan A was not going to work. At three of the locations the EXPO found that the material started heating up very quickly and smoking once he started to move it. The conclusion everyone reached at each place was the same – this looked like a thermal reaction of the chemicals involved. It was getting very hot and we all knew the reaction could accelerate. It underlined that this was a highly volatile and dangerous material – in fact the most sensitive improvised explosive that I ever came across during my years at the FEL.

A thermal reaction is not the same as an explosion – it is slower, but it can be extremely violent and produce massive heat in a split second. I was very aware of the danger because I knew of two separate incidents at the Fort – in different departments to the FEL – when uncontrolled thermal reactions had killed one person and, in the other case, left someone with life-changing burn injuries.

'Okay, stop. Stop,' I said, during a phone call to one of the locations to discuss this. 'We can't do this – we are going to need another plan.'

It was a tricky time to make clear decisions. I had senior police officers in one ear saying 'Tell us what this stuff is, Cliff, and get it cleaned up and out of the way so we can reopen the transport network', while, in the other, I had case officers telling me it was too dangerous to move. And by this time it was getting late and we were all knackered. I'd been on the go all day in Leeds and had then come down to London and I was feeling the pace. I was also very aware that people in our line of work need their wits about them and silly mistakes could happen when working with unpredictable substances when people are exhausted. So just before midnight I told everyone to stand down and go and get some sleep – we would tackle this in the morning, and London and the Met would have to wait.

It's decision that I am happy to stand by. Of course there was enormous pressure to get the stations back open and return the capital to something like normality, but my duty was to my staff and I remember thinking at the time that I would rather risk the wrath of a few senior police officers and politicians than the safety of my case officers.

21/7 – detonators but no bombs

I went home from the Fort and grabbed some shut-eye. At just before 4 a.m. my phone sprang to life and I awoke from a fitful sleep with a start.

'Cliff, it's Jim Edmonds [not his real name] from New Scotland Yard . . .'

I swallowed hard. 'Hi, Jim . . . it's er . . . 03.57 . . . and I am . . .'

'I know . . . I need to know why everything has stopped at the scenes. What's going on? We have to have everything working again by the morning rush hour . . .'

'Well, Jim, it has stopped because the stuff is reacting . . .'

'Yeah, okay, but you've just got to move it . . .'

'Look, it's dangerous, we're not really sure what it is and we all very tired, including me; we'll think again in the morning.'

'Not good enough, Cliff . . . the whole of f***in' London is waiting for you guys to do your jobs . . .'

He couldn't exactly order me to get back to work, but I realised I needed to sound at the very least co-operative. 'Okay, look, I hear you, I hear you; I will go and see the EXPO guys first thing and we will come up with a new plan,' I said.

I sat on the bed feeling the pressure. Suddenly it had come down to me to sort out this mess and London was waiting. Not for the first time in my working life I surveyed my career and wondered how I had managed to end up being in charge of my department when nothing of the sort had ever been my intention. Now I could really feel the weight of responsibility that came with it; Londoners were dependent on my decision-making for their stations to be opened again and my instinct was to take as long as necessary.

I couldn't sleep after that. I got dressed and, as dawn was breaking, I drove to the Fort. There I found the case officer who had been at the Oval and had managed to get her stuff back in a police van without it either heating up or smoking. We went to the store and had a look at it together. At that stage I was still assuming it was probably a similar mix to the 7/7 bomb material – hydrogen peroxide and pepper.

Then I hopped on the train at Orpington and headed into town to meet the EXPOs at their headquarters at Canon Row police station. We needed to come up with Plan B, and while we were working on it the news came through that a suspect had been shot and killed by police at Stockwell Underground station in south London. An EXPO was scrambled to check the body for explosives but there were none. This later turned out to be the death of an entirely innocent 27-year-old Brazilian man, Jean Charles de Menezes, who had been mistaken by the police for one of the bombers.

That shooting was an absolute tragedy that occurred during a particularly fraught time in London as the hunt for the would-be bombers of 21/7 continued. Inevitably, the police came in for much criticism for what they did that morning, but I have always believed that the people who were really responsible for the death of Mr de Menezes were the bombers. In my view, he was the sole victim of their failed attacks the previous day.

With the response to the events at Stockwell playing out around us at Canon Row, we devised a slightly different approach. This time the EXPOs would not try to move the mixture in a big lump but spread it out and then cut the nylon bags open and try to slide it section by section, or blob by blob, on to the bags. Once they had done that the bags would be sealed with tape and then placed in the plastic boxes, which would be filled with a couple of inches in depth of cold water.

My thinking was that, if the mix started reacting again, it would melt the plastic and then dilute and cool again when it came into contact with the water. Those boxes would be taken to the fire training area at Biggin Hill airport, not far from the FEL south of London, where they would be burnt.

The final part of the plan was that at each location the EXPO should take a separate small sample of around 200g of the mix. This should be boxed up on its own, also in water, and taken by police vans to the FEL for use as test samples.

EXPLOSIVE

It sounds simple enough but the process we had outlined took almost all day. At one of the locations – Shepherd's Bush – the main bulk of the material proved so unstable that, early in the evening, the EXPO abandoned the plan and removed it to a green space nearby where he burnt it himself.

But we were making progress. I drove to Biggin Hill to see the stuff from Warren Street and the bus at Bethnal Green. It was well spread out, had stopped reacting and burned away in a controlled manner, which was reassuring. I headed back to the lab to await the arrival of the final sample, which was being driven in a police van from Shepherd's Bush.

Then my phone rang.

'Cliff, Cliff, the samples are fizzing and bubbling and the van is filling up with smoke.'

It was an exhibits officer from the anti-terrorist branch and I could hear the rising panic in his voice.

Although this was a small amount of a much larger bomb, it was still capable of creating a significant explosion. Along with the policemen driving, the officer had his own life to consider as well as anyone else using the roads and pavements in the parts of London they were moving through.

'What do we do? What do we do?' he was asking.

'Hang on a second,' I said, as a vision of a police van

blowing up on a busy London street briefly invaded my subconscious.

I considered calling an EXPO and telling the police officers to stop so we could try to make the sample safe or even burn it there and then. But, eventually, after getting a bit more visual detail from them on what was happening, I agreed with their own suggestion that they should continue. The material had calmed down a bit and they decided to carry on and just try to get to the Fort as fast as possible. We agreed that if it started to deteriorate again then they should find a suitable place to stop.

I called the Ministry of Defence police at the main gate and told them that a police van was approaching with a small but highly unstable cargo of explosives. They were not to stop it under any circumstances and forgo their usual practice of signing every vehicle in. Instead this van was to proceed straight to a designated area where we could unload the package and try to tamp the mix down.

The van duly sped through the gates and we got the package into a large container full of water and then began dividing the sample into even smaller amounts until it all calmed down and we were able to take a collective deep breath.

The van had broken all the rules on entry and we had broken most of our own protocols on how to handle unclassified improvised-explosive material. But in those frantic days immediately after 21/7, the rulebook on material handling and health and safety at the FEL went out of the window as we raced to deal with a complex and rapidly changing situation.

To their credit, my senior managers at the Defence Science and Technology Laboratory (Dstl) left me to get on with it, much as we had agreed they would when I took the job as head of department. I only heard from one of them once, who told me simply: 'Tell us what you need and we will get it for you.' Thankfully, this was a far cry from the days of the Lockerbie style of macho management.

At this point the police made the decision to split the two investigations – 7/7 and 21/7 – into two, which made life a lot simpler for all of us involved. It meant we could effectively put 7/7 on hold and just focus on 21/7, which was far more urgent, given that the perpetrators were still at large.

The smoking van was followed two days after the attacks by the discovery in Little Wormwood Scrubs Park in west London of a fifth device, which had been abandoned without any attempt to detonate it. Once again in this situation I could only admire the courage and professionalism of the EXPO at the scene who manually dismantled the device and separated out the detonator from the rest of the material (which wasn't reacting), so we could establish exactly what this gang had used to initiate their bombs.

The detonator consisted of a roll of card wrapped up in masking tape and filled with a white powder and with an electric match head on a wire inserted at one end that was connected to a battery. The EXPO soaked the roll in an alcohol and water solution and then cut into the card with a scalpel and extracted some of the powder. Unlike at 7/7, it turned out not to be HMTD but its detonating bedfellow, TATP.

The find of a fifth bomb was followed two days later by the discovery of a bomb factory in a council flat where one of the suspects had been living in north London. It was there that police found buckets with residues of gloop and bags of chapatti flour, and it became clear that, instead of pepper and hydrogen peroxide, these bombers had used flour as the fuel. It was another new al-Qaeda combination for us to get our heads around.

By the end of that momentous month in 2005, the police had arrested all four of the main suspects, three in England and one in Rome, where he was awaiting extradition. Our job by then was to concentrate on demonstrating that the mix they had used was a viable explosive and that their bombs could have gone off, which was obviously critical to their successful prosecution on charges of attempted murder. And the find of the fifth device was our first lucky break in this case, which provided us with the means to do this very effectively.

In the days following the fraught arrival of the van with smoking samples, our problems with the gloop did not go away. Although we had stopped them reacting any further by cooling them down and dividing them, a check the following day showed that some had started reacting again.

I now had yet another serious decision to make. The best way to show that this material was a viable explosive was to use a Gap test – the same procedure we had used with the IRA lorry bomb found at Stoke Newington in 1992. But this required at least 200g of material. We had more than enough to do this, but now that some of it had started reacting again, I felt I had no choice but to get rid of most of it because it was simply too dangerous to keep.

So the find of the fifth device now proved a godsend; it gave us enough stable material to do one test, if we were quick about it. The test consists of putting a sample of the material into a steel tube, which is placed upright on a steel plate. An explosive charge is then placed on the top of the tube and then the mixture is 'fired'. All the fragments of the tube and plate are then collected and photographed and compared with the results of the same process, first, when an inert material like sand is used, and then when different types of known explosives are used. Finally we had our answer: the test proved that the mixture was certainly a viable explosive.

For prosecution counsel, however, this was not the end of the matter. It was clear that the devices had not exploded properly, but they needed to show in court that this was a mistake by the bombers, not a deliberate act. In order to answer this question, several large explosives trials were needed. This was not something that the FEL could do, but there was a sister department within Dstl at the Fort that did precisely this work. So it was easy for me to just go and talk to those colleagues on site and, with management's help, get this all set up.

In the months that followed, a whole series of explosives trials were carried out showing how the flour and hydrogen peroxide mix did or did not work so well, depending on the degree of concentration of hydrogen peroxide, the balance of the mix between flour and hydrogen peroxide and the amount of detonating high explosive used. We showed that the gang had got their mixture slightly wrong but that their intention was clearly to detonate their devices in full and kill themselves and everyone else around them, not just scare people out of their wits.

The four bombers, Muktar Said Ibrahim (twenty-nine), Yasin Hassan Omar (twenty-six), Ramzi Mohammed (twenty-five) and Hussain Osman (twenty-eight) had all come to Britain as refugees from war-torn countries in the Horn of Africa. They had carried out their attacks in protest at Britain's role in the war and occupation of Iraq. They were each sentenced to life with a minimum of forty years' imprisonment in July 2007 after a five-and-a-half-month trial at Woolwich Crown Court.

I was impressed that the prosecution decided to go for conspiracy to murder, with a much higher burden of proof required than prosecuting them for possession of explosives under the Explosive Substances Act 1883. That would have got them fifteen years without much difficulty, but the Crown barristers wanted to nail this group of Islamic extremists for their real intentions on 21/7 and feared that a jury might convict only for possession if given the choice and baulk at attempted murder.

The fifth member of the gang, the Ghanaian-born Manfo Asiedu (thirty-four), who had abandoned his device at Little Wormwood Scrubs after losing his nerve, was jailed for thirty-three years, four months after his accomplices.

This had been another hugely exhausting and time-consuming case for all of us at the FEL and I, for one, was delighted to see that an attempt to successfully appeal their conviction at the Court of Appeal in 2008 was rejected, as was a subsequent appeal at the European Court of Human Rights.

The attempt by counsel for the men at the Court of Appeal to argue that their devices were made to look realistic 'but included flaws which had been built into them to ensure that the main charge of each of the devices would not detonate' was patently ridiculous. I had no doubt in my mind that if the bombers had got their mix right, we would have witnessed an atrocity that was as shocking as, if not worse than, what had happened on 7/7.

At the Court of Appeal, Sir Igor Judge, who was sitting with two other appeal judges, was spot on when he told the defendants: 'These were merciless and extreme crimes. As they were rightly meant to be, the sentences were severe and extreme. Beyond doubt, however, they were utterly justified.'

21

The first bombers to use liquid explosive

On the evening of 31 July 2006, I was writing up my notes on a new case we had opened at the FEL during what was probably the most intensely busy phase of activity that I ever saw at the Fort. We were running a number of simultaneous investigations and case files, not the least of which was our preparation for the upcoming trial of the 21/7 bombers.

That day we had received one or two items from SO15, the Met's renamed anti-terrorist branch, who informed us that this was more evidence they had recovered during a long-running surveillance operation that was being conducted jointly with MI5 into a possible bomb plot. The items we received were curious more than sinister.

In one consignment there were some small bulbs that you might find lighting a Christmas tree. But these ones had had their glass envelopes cut off. We established, through microscopic analysis, that the bulbs were coated in tiny grains of manganese, zinc and potassium chloride, the internal contents of a battery that might be used in a torch. That seemed somewhat odd and not necessarily potentially explosive.

The other package we were sent that day contained some samples that had been seized covertly during the operation. There were a cotton wool ball, a cotton bud and a solution in a small bottle with a yellowish gelatinised lump in the bottom of it.

The SO15 guys were working in those days, as we all were, in the knowledge that hydrogen peroxide – which, as we have seen, is a clear caustic liquid used as a bleach and as a dye by hairdressers – had been a key ingredient in the bombs on 7/7, and they wanted to know if there was any trace of it on these items.

Three weeks earlier they had sent us swab samples from two buildings near Heathrow, and some latex gloves they had found, asking the same question. On that occasion our tests proved negative and they were negative on these items too; the solution in the bottle was not hydrogen peroxide but a mixture of starch, glucose and water.

I had picked up the vibes from the SO15 officers that this operation was potentially a biggie. In fact this would be the most extensive covert police surveillance operation in British criminal history, involving hundreds of officers and costing tens of millions of pounds. But, for us at least, it had small beginnings.

That night I finished detailing the work we had completed and then signed off the entry with two comments: 'Need more samples. Seems case might grow.'

If only I could have known, because, a week later, when the principal suspects in what became known as the 'Airlines Plot' were suddenly arrested, we were deluged in samples and investigative work. It would become one of the most demanding cases ever dealt with at the FEL, generating more than eighty separate case files.

This was a conspiracy to blow up transatlantic aircraft using suicide bombers that changed airline travel for all of us, just as the Shoe Bomber case had before it. This one made its presence felt on the general public with the abrupt imposition of new restrictions on the amount of liquid you could take in hand luggage on to an aircraft. The restrictions, which are still in place today and are likely to remain so for ever more, caused weeks of chaos at security gates as airports struggled to carry out new checks without causing long delays.

In forensic terms it was an unprecedented case: a conspiracy that utilised a liquid explosive mixture, something that had never been tried, or planned, in a serious and deadly way before. It was also unique in the way the bombers planned to take the *components* of a bomb through airport security, not a fully made-up device. Almost all of these were harmless in themselves, but they could quickly be assembled on board to create a device that had the potential to bring a passenger jet down. This too had never been seen before.

In terms of the evolution of our work at the FEL, this case illustrates the way it had developed from the era dominated by the IRA. By the end of their thirty-year campaign, both in Northern Ireland and on the British mainland, we had become well acquainted with their methods and techniques and it was relatively rare for us to be genuinely surprised by what we were presented with, from a technical point of view.

Islamic extremist terrorist groups – and particularly al-Qaeda-influenced cells – were quite different in this respect. Each case would present us with new chemical combinations and new packaging and concealment methods. We had to learn to keep an open mind about what we were dealing with and think hard about how it might all work.

The arrest of eight suspects a week after I wrote that fateful entry in my case notes followed the intervention of our friends in America. They had grown increasingly nervous that MI5 and SO15 were allowing the plot, which was based in London, to run too far before stepping in and stopping it. They were terrified that another massive terrorist attack could happen, involving up to seven aircraft and causing potentially thousands of deaths, many of them American citizens, and giving al-Qaeda its biggest success since 9/11.

EXPLOSIVE

The plot was being masterminded by Rashid Rauf, a Birmingham-born British Muslim living in Pakistan, who was in regular contact with the cell in London. Rauf was detained by the Pakistanis after they were prompted to move on him by impatient senior US officials. His arrest forced SO15's hand. Once they knew he was in custody, they had only a matter of hours to respond if the plotters were not to realise that their game was up and either start destroying evidence or even launch an attack.

The subsequent arrests, almost all of them in London, produced a huge amount of work for us. All the suspects had to be checked for traces of explosives on their hands and clothes, and all their homes, cars and any other premises they were using had to be checked and tested.

At the same time the police were trying to piece together what exactly the plotters were intending to do. For all of us on the investigative side, this turned out to be a journey of discovery in which we first pieced together how their bombs would work and then identified the targets.

In the wake of the arrests, the police sent us samples of a liquid and a compound they had seized at one of the addresses. They asked us a simple question. Could these be mixed together to make an explosive? The liquid was our old friend hydrogen peroxide and the substance had been identified as Tang powder, the key ingredient in artificial orange drink, which is normally mixed with water.

As we have seen throughout this book, for an explosive

mixture you need an oxidiser and a fuel. On 7/7 the bombers had used hydrogen peroxide as their oxidiser and ground black pepper as the fuel; on 21/7 hydrogen peroxide had been mixed with flour. In each case the proportions had been calculated carefully to achieve the desired explosive effect (although the 21/7 gang didn't quite get it right).

Tang powder and hydrogen peroxide were a new combination and the best way to assess its explosive significance – if it had any – was to conduct what we called a 'cartridge case test'. This was an old routine that involved placing a small amount of a mixture in an empty .303 rifle cartridge case made of copper and nickel. You then inserted a detonator into the mixture and electrically 'fired' the charge to create an explosion with the cartridge case safely held inside a steel retaining case. You could then assess what sort of damage to the cartridge case was caused and compare that to other substances, using pictures of earlier tests that we had on file.

Once again, the police wanted an answer urgently. The cartridge case test was rarely used and I was one of the few people at the lab still qualified to do it. Since time was of the essence, I decided to do it myself and I quickly encountered a problem. The test was intended to be used only with solid materials, not with a liquid, and it was hard to see how to make it work with hydrogen peroxide and Tang.

I tried inserting a small plastic fitting from a laboratory liquid dispenser into the casing. The aim was to try to stop the mixture leaking out of the hole in the base of the cartridge where the primer cap normally goes when a cartridge is loaded for firing in a rifle. But that did not work. Then I resorted to cling film. After one or two false starts, I managed to make a tiny pouch, which I filled with the liquid mix using a syringe, and then carefully pushed it into the casing. It was the best I could do.

I inserted a small commercial detonator and fired the mixture. After working my way through various small modifications, and after experimenting with different proportions of the ingredients, I got it to work to my satisfaction. I had a result: *Bang!* . . . a mixture of artificial flavouring for orange drink and hair dye could potentially form a viable explosive. I was impressed. It was a finding that would lie at the heart of the Crown's case against the plotters.

The chemistry of this unlikely explosive was simple enough. When the detonator fired, it sent a shock wave through the mixture that produced a very fast reaction between the Tang and the hydrogen peroxide. This, in turn, produced a rapidly-expanding – and very hot – gas, which, as it forced its way out of confinement, destroyed the cartridge casing. The effect was a proper explosion that shredded the casing. It was what we would term a 'middling detonating velocity explosive' – similar to something like gelignite.

The cartridge case test is a reliable one, but it is not enough on its own to form the basis for a firm conclusion that would stand up in court, because it is conducted on such a small scale with perhaps only 2g of testing material. The police wanted to know if it could be done on a larger scale and asked one of their EXPOs to carry out a similar exercise, but with about 100g of liquid.

The officer got on the phone to me and told me what they wanted and I could tell that he was not keen. I cautioned him not to do it – it was potentially dangerous and could be done by Dstl in a more scientifically rigorous manner. We agreed that the larger format would be better set up at the Fort by the department that specialises in conducting explosives trials for the Ministry of Defence. It took them about four weeks to work their way through it, using a steel tube with a plastic base glued to the bottom of it to contain the liquid.

The results were conclusive; as the cartridge test had demonstrated, in the right proportions, the mixture of Tang powder and hydrogen peroxide could make a reliable explosive. Those early tests commissioned for this case formed the beginning of a much bigger research programme into hydrogen peroxide explosive mixtures that was carried out at the Fort.

In the meantime the flood of work associated with this case continued to flow in, and before long almost every senior case officer at the FEL – eight in all, plus four or five less-experienced ones – were involved. We were dealing with hundreds of separate exhibits recovered from six main addresses and locations, including two areas of woodland. Every address had been searched and any materials or documents with even a remote possibility of being linked to explosive preparation had to be analysed and tested.

Initially I thought I could co-ordinate the case myself, but, with all my other responsibilities, it soon became clear that this was not realistic. Instead I asked Kenneth Hales to take charge of it. He had the advantage of having been away from the FEL during the initial investigations into 7/7 and 21/7 and was thus less over-committed than almost everyone else. He was a good choice and handled a complex assignment adroitly.

The next consignment was a collection of AA batteries that had been found six days after the arrests. The EXPO on scene had spotted a very small gap in the casings of the batteries and, using remote handling machinery, had managed to X-ray them. These showed that each one contained a small light bulb – just what you would expect if the batteries were being used as detonators.

Once we got hold of them, we X-rayed them ourselves and confirmed his finding. Now we understood the significance of the Christmas tree bulbs and the explanation for the residue of battery contents that we had found on them. We had the batteries opened at another part of the Fort and discovered another curiosity in this case; they were not filled with an explosive substance but, in one case, sugar and, in another, salt. We concluded that these were dummies perhaps intended for a dry run-through in an airport to make sure that they would get through security scanners unnoticed.

As the case developed, our task at the FEL was to demonstrate for the prosecution how the bomb in this well-organised plot would work. The police had surveillance video showing the leading figure in the group, Abdulla Ahmed Ali, examining Oasis plastic soft drinks bottles in a local corner store. They also had video of the plotters drilling a hole in the bottom of one of these bottles in a house they were using as a bomb factory and draining the contents. This was clever because the top seal on the bottle remained undisturbed while the tiny hole in the base could later be re-closed with a blob of nearly colourless glue.

We needed to show that once refilled with a mixture of Tang and hydrogen peroxide, which looked similar to an Oasis orange drink, the improvised detonator contained in the battery would function and was capable of igniting the mixture in the bottle. In addition to the naked filament of the bulb, the battery would need a sensitive primary explosive that could be ignited by transmitting an electric current to the filament through two wires that could be stored in the battery while it was in transit through security.

The gang had never got round to making HMTD, which was an ideal choice, but the ingredients for it, along with recipes and instructions on how to make it, had been found at their bomb factory. It seemed pretty clear that

HMTD was on their minds. We set up various experiments with the Tang and hydrogen peroxide mixture and detonators, in containers similar to the batteries they had prepared. They demonstrated that an AA-sized detonator was capable of initiating the bomb.

It did so when the battery was taped to the side of the Oasis bottle but worked even more effectively when the battery was immersed in the liquid through the opened top cap. This could then be screwed down with the wires still protruding for connection to a trigger battery. All this could either be done by a suicide bomber sitting in his seat on the aircraft or perhaps during a visit to the toilet on board.

There is no doubt that this was an ingenious device that had been cooked up somewhere in Pakistan or perhaps Afghanistan at an al-Qaeda training camp. What struck me about it was its versatility in terms of how easily it could be transported in a deconstructed state and the likelihood that it would have got through airport security undetected. It was also notable for its use of common household products to create a potentially devastating bomb on an aircraft. The question was, however, just how likely was it that one of these devices would cause a plane to fall out of the sky?

Research on the internet by the plotters on flight times suggested they were planning to carry seven bombs on to seven different flights from Heathrow to cities in North America – San Francisco, Toronto, Montreal, Washington,

The first bombers to use liquid explosive

New York and Chicago. All the flights were scheduled to depart within two and a half hours of each other, so that once the first of the bombs had gone off over the Atlantic – or even over the American coast – the other planes would be too far out to get back over land before they too were blown up.

At the FEL we could not say for certain whether the bombs would be capable of bringing a plane down. We conducted tests that were filmed from several angles and demonstrated that they were capable of creating sizeable explosions. The BBC also commissioned a demonstration using an old aeroplane fuselage that had been recovered from a scrapyard. A drinks bottle bomb was placed in front of a row of seats and then detonated. It caused devastating damage to the interior of the plane and a large, gaping hole in the wall of the fuselage itself. We knew from what had happened over Lockerbie that this could have been enough to bring a plane down.

But, in our evidence to the court, we cautioned that the effectiveness of a bomb would depend on a range of factors, as Kenneth explained in his statement at trial. 'Would such a device bring down an aircraft in flight? I can't say for sure,' he wrote. 'There are too many unknown variables, such as the model of aircraft, the position of the bomb in the plane, the altitude and air pressure at the time and so on. What we can say – based on common

297

sense – is that exploding one or more of these bombs on a commercial aircraft in flight wouldn't do the plane any good and I wouldn't want to be on it.'

There is no doubt that the British authorities would have preferred the plot to have run on for a few more hours or perhaps even a couple more days, had the Americans not forced their hand. This almost certainly made convictions that much harder to secure in a conspiracy case when almost all the suspects had recorded suicide videos but no attack had actually taken place and no complete bombs had been assembled.

After an initial trial in the summer of 2008, three men – Ali, Assad Sarwar and Tanvir Hussain – were convicted at Woolwich Crown Court of plotting to kill 'persons unknown'. But following six weeks of deliberation, the jury failed to reach a verdict on their role in orchestrating an airline bomb plot, which I found extremely disappointing. Another suspect was cleared of all charges, while the jury failed to reach verdicts on three other men.

Two years later the three convicted at the first trial were convicted after a retrial on the airline plot charges. Ali, who had warned the British public to expect 'floods of martyr operations' in his video and had considered taking his baby son with him on his suicide mission, was jailed for a minimum of forty years. On his arrest police had found an elaborate blueprint for the plot scrawled in a battered pocket diary. Sarwar was given a minimum of thirty-six years, while Hussain was ordered to be detained for a minimum of thirty-two years.

Although others were acquitted, I was pleased with the outcome. There was no doubt in my mind what this gang had intended to do and they had gone about it with a level of aptitude and application that made them highly dangerous. I wasn't in the least bit surprised when the new restrictions on liquids in hand luggage came in – it was the least the authorities could do to ensure that this particular variation on the suicide bombing of a passenger jet never comes to pass.

The Airlines Plot took its toll on all of us at the lab, not least me. I am sure the strain of it affected me and my relationship with Vanessa, because, along with the trials for 7/7 and 21/7, with which it overlapped, work seemed to occupy most of my time and attention for probably more than three years, from July 2005 through to 2008. For much of that time she had been recovering after being diagnosed with breast cancer in 2004, and although I did try to be around as much as possible for her through that, I feel now I probably should have done more. Certainly, when the OBE popped up for the 2009 New Year's honours list, my immediate (and abiding) thought was that this would be a good reward for Vanessa, for all my general lack of attention, with a visit to the palace, and she did love all of that. But there was far too little awareness on my part of the toll this was all taking on both of us, and, to cap it all, over the winter of 2009/2010, I took a four-month assignment as 'scientific liaison' to Task Force Helmand (the British army) in Afghanistan, and it was particularly hard on Vanessa.

In that assignment, I was the senior Dstl person at the main British base at Camp Bastion. It was non-stop work helping to sort out technical issues with army kit and doing my bit on the personnel front to assist the fifteen or so other Dstl people out there. I was lucky. I got to live in a portable cabin, not a tent.

I went there because I felt I should do my bit and because I knew the MoD was finding it hard to fill the post on a voluntary basis. Although I was never on the front line, I did visit our troops at one forward base – at Lashkar Gah – and spent some time at the base at Kandahar, but I was only ever under attack by rocket or shellfire once, and the rounds came in a long way from me.

When I got back to the FEL, where my duties had been shared by two or three of my colleagues, I gave them a briefing on what I had been up to, partly in the hope that it might encourage others to follow my example. I remember one chap at the lab asking me whether I thought it was a mistake that we were even in Afghanistan. My answer was maybe, maybe not.

I reckoned it would all depend on whether we could establish the Afghan National Army as a viable and robust force that could operate anywhere in the country without external support. While the police were hopelessly vulnerable to intimidation and attack by Taliban guerrillas, because they worked in their own local areas and therefore could be recognised, the army largely did not. I have to say I was sceptical about the future, and what has happened since I was there – sadly – seems to have justified that scepticism. If he had asked that same question of me on a personal level, with hindsight I would have to say – yes, it was.

22

Benazir Bhutto – when a bomb- and bullet-proof car is not enough

During my years at the FEL, I got used to travelling abroad to countries that were facing a major national crisis as a result of a bombing or were coping with the aftermath of a disaster like a plane crash.

But by the far the most febrile atmosphere I encountered on any of these trips was on my last working assignment in a foreign setting, when two colleagues and I travelled to Pakistan in the wake of the assassination of the former prime minister Benazir Bhutto.

Her death at the age of fifty-four, alongside twenty-three others in a gun and suicide bomb attack as she left a political rally in Rawalpindi in December 2007, had stunned Pakistan and was followed by widespread rioting, amid anger directed at the government of President Pervez Musharraf.

The protests claimed the lives of at least forty-seven people and caused extensive damage to property, including

302

railway stations, banks and shops, especially in her home province of Sind and its capital, Karachi.

During our week-long stay in the country, we were more or less restricted to the grounds of our hotel in Islamabad, and whenever we ventured out we were accompanied by police pick-ups full of armed officers in front of and behind our armoured car, while other units cleared the traffic ahead.

It never particularly bothered me having all that sort of security and the implication that our lives were in constant danger. I did not consider myself and my colleagues – Helen Jones and Sheila Davies – to be targets. I'd been to Pakistan before, lecturing to police units on explosives forensics, and had a sense of how life there ebbed and flowed. True, they had a major national crisis on their hands, but this was an argument between themselves, not with us.

What I will always remember about that trip was a moment during our examination of the Toyota Land Cruiser that Ms Bhutto had been travelling in when she was killed. This vehicle, and what happened in its immediate vicinity at the entrance to Liaquat National Bagh, a public park in Rawalpindi, was already the subject of intense speculation and conflicting theories about how exactly the former prime minister had died.

I couldn't help thinking, as I stood in the yard at Rawalpindi Police Lines looking at the scarred panelling of the

Toyota, just how unlucky Benazir Bhutto had been. The armoured vehicle was in a pretty poor state but it had done its job superbly well and yet she had managed to meet her death in any case – it seemed as if fate or destiny had made it certain that she would not survive that day.

The call to go to Pakistan came from our colleagues at SO15, who had been assisting the Pakistani authorities with the investigation into the assassination. We were asked to attend along with the UK pathologist Dr Nathaniel Cary and a doctor from Porton Down. Between us, we were to produce a report into the murder for the British government that would also be shared with the government of Pakistan.

I got the sense that Whitehall wanted its own straightforward account of what had happened that might cut through all the sound and fury coming out of Pakistan itself.

Primarily SO15 wanted answers to two questions. How many attackers had there been and what was the cause of Ms Bhutto's death? With the British government already providing assistance in a general way to Pakistan, with various advisers and security experts, there was ready funding from the Foreign Office for our trip, and I took advantage by taking two colleagues with me, not just one, as was normally the case.

When I explained to senior officers at SO15 that Helen would be the nominated FEL case officer while Sheila would be coming along to gain valuable experience on what was an unusually sensitive foreign assignment, there were one or two raised eyebrows.

'Cliff, you do realise Pakistan is an Islamic country and they are not used to dealing with women in positions of authority?'

'Yes, I know that,' I agreed, 'but until last week there was every possibility they were going to re-elect a woman as their prime minister. In any case, I am sure this will not be an issue – it's not Saudi Arabia.'

To be fair, I was allowed to get on with it and my confidence in this respect was largely well-placed. However, I did smile ruefully during our first big briefing with senior Pakistani police officers and security officials in Islamabad, which took place on the day we arrived, ten days after the assassination.

Some of the officers were quite happy to address Helen directly – others did so but then seemed to defer to me after each exchange, looking in my general direction as if for my approval or endorsement of what she had said.

'You heard it from Helen,' I would say. 'I have nothing to add. If you have any further questions, please feel free to follow up with her.'

On the day she died, Ms Bhutto had addressed a large rally of her supporters – most of them members of the opposition Pakistan People's Party – who had been corralled in a controlled area inside the park. She gave an impassioned speech railing at the inadequacies and corruption of the government of General Musharraf, almost all of it at the top of her voice in a rasping and hoarse delivery by a woman who seemed exhausted by the demands of the election campaign.

When it was time to leave, a bespectacled and smiling Ms Bhutto, dressed in a purple one-piece outfit and with her head draped in a white scarf, made her way through the crowd to her armoured Land Cruiser, which was waiting to take her out of the park in convoy with several other vehicles.

As far as we could tell from our briefing with the Pakistani police, the movement in and out of the park had been the subject of quite intense pre-event planning. Everyone knew that Ms Bhutto was a major security risk, with many of her supporters convinced that the government itself would be prepared to see her killed. She had returned from eight years in self-imposed exile in Britain and Dubai to Pakistan only a couple of months earlier. On the day she arrived she had survived a double suicide bomb attack while travelling in convoy into Karachi that had killed 130 people and injured 500 others but left her unscathed.

On this occasion she was to remain inside her armoured Toyota and the driver was told not to stop under any circumstances as the convoy made its way out of the controlled zone of the park and then through a crowd of well-wishers who had gathered outside.

What actually happened was not what had been planned. We were told that Ms Bhutto was determined to wave to her supporters, who had not been able to attend her speech, and she may have instructed the driver to slow down or even stop as the Toyota made its way through the crowd outside the park.

She then stood up on the back seat and appeared with her upper body projecting through an escape hatch in the roof of the Land Cruiser, the better to wave at, and greet, her supporters. At the same time the now motionless vehicle became entirely surrounded by the crowd. It was exactly the situation that her security advisers had hoped to avoid.

It was at this moment that up to three shots were fired and then immediately afterwards a bomb was detonated right next to the vehicle by an individual wearing a suicide vest packed with explosives and ball bearings. In videos of the attack, Benazir Bhutto can be seen ducking down as the shots ring out and then the fireball of the blast engulfs the screen.

What we knew was that an unconscious Bhutto was then rushed to Rawalpindi General Hospital, arriving at 17.35 local time, and that she died there at 18.16. Her body was almost immediately removed by her family for burial in her home village in Sind and no autopsy was ever carried out.

In the hours and days afterwards, the row over exactly what had happened to her erupted and intensified. The

Pakistan Interior Ministry initially said she had died as a result of a skull fracture caused by her head striking the frame of the escape hatch, as the Land Cruiser rocked violently from side to side under the impact of the blast wave. This was rejected by her own aides, who said she had suffered two gunshot wounds prior to the bombing and that these may have killed her.

It was an intense and continually developing story. I found it extraordinary that Bhutto's supporters seemed to require her to have died heroically in order to be a proper martyr to her cause. Being shot seemed to fit that bill, whereas striking her head on the edge of a hatch in the roof of a Land Cruiser did not.

It was against that background that we went to examine the Land Cruiser and the other vehicles from the convoy at the police compound in Rawalpindi. Sheila, Helen and I spent many hours studying the vehicle, and what became clear to us was that the armour plating and armoured glass in the windows had done a very effective job.

I could find no evidence that any shrapnel – or the remains of steel ball bearings – had penetrated the inside of the Land Cruiser. The outer bodywork on the rear nearside close to where the bomb had detonated was pockmarked with hundreds of impacts but nothing had got through the armour plating that had been added on the inside.

We examined the interior of the vehicle carefully to assess whether anything could have been cleared up before we got there, but there were no signs of holes in the fabric of the car. Outside we had a section of the bodywork cut out so we could examine debris that had been trapped between the outer panelling and the armour plating – the crushed remnants of ball bearings – and it was clear that nothing had penetrated further than that.

The Land Cruiser was severely damaged and the whole side of the vehicle had been pushed in and scorched by the blast, but it had not caught fire. You could sense from the extent of the damage just how violent the rocking motion would have been as the vehicle bounced on its suspension under the intense forces of a bomb that had been detonated just a few feet away.

Although the British doctor from Porton Down and Dr Cary had not been able to examine or even see the body, they saw X-rays taken of Benazir Bhutto's head, which they showed me. A fracture along the right side of her skull was clearly visible and it was consistent with her having hit it on the side of the escape hatch. The X-rays showed no sign of bullet impacts in her head.

Of course I was aware that this vehicle was at the centre of a national crisis, and that it was the setting for the fatal injury to a global figure, a woman who had led Pakistan through two terms as prime minister. On the right-hand seat in the back, bloodstains were still clearly visible where Benazir had fallen down after being fatally injured. But it would be wrong to say that I was overly concerned about the 'human' aspect of what I was looking at. Once again, it may sound coldly professional, but to me this was just another vehicle that had been in a bombing and I had a job to do trying to work out what I could tell the people who had sent me there and whose questions we were trying to answer.

In that respect I guess I was no different from pathologists who put the human element out of their mind when they open up a body, or paramedics when they collect up human remains after a bombing. They are not thinking about the people or the families involved; they are doing their job to the best of their ability, and I was doing just that in Rawalpindi.

After we had finished our work on the Toyota, we asked if we could see the scene of the bombing, even if our expectations of finding anything useful there were extremely low. This was because the Pakistani authorities had immediately swept and then hosed down the area where the bomb had gone off, leaving almost nothing of value from a forensic point of view.

As we prepared to visit Liaquat National Bagh – again with a heavy armed escort – I got a call from a member of Dstl's more senior management, fairly new in his post, who had decided to intervene.

'You're going to the scene, Cliff?' he said.

'Yes, that's the idea.'

'Oh well, I'm not sure that all of you should do that. It might be safer for just two of you to go, don't you agree?'

'No, I don't, as a matter of fact,' I told him. 'We have all come out here to do this job and it would be nuts for one of us to stay behind. Besides, we are probably just as safe at the scene as we would be at the hotel, so it makes no difference.'

'I'll come back to you on this,' he said, and I waited an hour or so before the phone rang again.

'Hi, Cliff, I've discussed this with my superiors,' he said, as I felt my heart sink. 'And we have unanimously decided that only two of you should go, on safety grounds.'

'Oh right . . . and which two?'

'Don't be silly, Cliff; it should be you and Helen, as the nominated case officer.'

I put the phone down feeling highly irritated. As far as I was concerned this was a typical example of unwonted and wrong-headed interference by well-meaning but rules-obsessed people back home who should have left us in the field to make decisions as we saw fit.

I went and talked it through with one of the senior SO15 officers. His view was that those on site were best placed to judge the security situation, echoing my own thoughts, so I decided to ignore the instructions from London. Then I discussed it with Helen and Sheila. I told them what had been said but explained I had no plans to accede to the request and they were delighted. 'Bollocks to that', was how I put it, I seem to remember.

At the scene there was precious little for us to see, as we had expected, apart from a pile of sweepings with odd bits of material and plastic, which were of little value. Of more interest were two darkish marks on the concrete slabs where the bombing had taken place. These were not craters, more scars from the blast, and they were consistent with it having been a suicide vest with the explosive packed into pouches in the front and the back but not in the sides, where the arms are.

In the event, the Pakistani police identified the bomber as a fifteen-year-old boy from Waziristan, and I was convinced that he had acted alone. On one of the videos you could see someone with a gun shooting, and seconds later the bomb explodes at almost exactly the same place. The police had recovered large parts of what they believed was the suicide bomber's body – his upper torso, legs and arms – but they never found another body with similar damage, which would have been the case had the bomber been an accomplice standing alongside the shooter.

We tried to do our work at the park, but it reminded me of the Lauda Air crash in Thailand, where forensic investigation was almost impossible because everything had been moved or even stolen. In this case the thorough clean-up and washing down of the hard standing had completely obliterated the evidence we needed. We did spend some time swabbing road signs and other surfaces, but they did not produce anything of significance.

Fortunately our colleagues at SO15 had managed to recover pieces of clothing from the scene earlier and we swabbed those and took the sample kits back to the FEL for analysis alongside samples we had taken from the cars in the compound (but not Bhutto's car, the side of which had been scorched by the explosion). These produced traces of RDX, TNT and PETN.

On that basis, we suggested the bomber had used hard blocks of a common military explosive called 'Composition B', or 'Comp B' as it is generally known. This is used in artillery shells, rockets, landmines and hand grenades. In its standard proportions it is made up of 59.4% RDX and 39.4% of TNT, with a small amount of paraffin wax to bind it together. The bomb was likely to have consisted of a few kilograms of explosive linked by detonating cord filled with PETN that would have been initiated by a handheld trigger device.

Our report contained plenty of caveats – there had been no extended and detailed search of the scene of the crime, no formal body recovery and identification procedure and no autopsy. Our medical team had had to rely heavily on the X-rays but these, at least, had been independently verified as being of Bhutto by comparison with her dental X-rays. They had also been able to talk to medical staff at the hospital who had been involved in her treatment, and to members of the Bhutto family, who had washed the body before burial.

Our team identified only one injury to the right side of Bhutto's head, and our medical guys were able to say categorically that this had not been caused by gunshot impacts. However, they could not rule out other injuries because the X-rays they saw were only of her head. Thus we had to say in the report that other injuries to the upper body or neck could not be completely ruled out.

But, in his section of the document, Dr Carey pronounced himself confident about the way she had died. 'The only tenable cause for the rapidly fatal head injury in this case is that it occurred as the result of impact due to the effects of the bomb blast,' he wrote. 'In my opinion, Mohtarma Benazir Bhutto died as a result of a severe head injury sustained as a consequence of the bomb blast and due to head impact somewhere in the escape hatch of the vehicle.'

I had little doubt that that was correct. Everything that I had seen was consistent with her having hit her head as a result of the forces unleashed by high explosive of a type that detonates at a velocity of between 6,000 and 9,000 metres a second in very close proximity to where she was standing in the Land Cruiser.

The key for me was that the X-rays of her head showed no evidence of bullet injury. Given that she was ducking her head as the bomb detonated – we could see that from the videos – it seemed highly unlikely that she would have suffered a bullet injury in either her neck or her upper body. While there was some blood on the seats consistent with a head injury, there did not appear to be as much as you might expect had she also suffered gunshot wounds to the neck or elsewhere.

We had done our best in difficult circumstances and with a scene that had been destroyed in forensic terms. The cars, though, gave up their secrets fairly readily. On an issue that has been shrouded in controversy and politically motivated manoeuvring ever since, I think our report was about as clear-cut as we could have managed.

It had been an interesting few days in Pakistan, but sitting on the BA flight back to Heathrow, I reached the conclusion that – with foreign assignments at least – it was now time for me to step back and let others take charge in the field.

In the years after that trip I focused almost entirely on my management duties as I prepared to hand over to my successor, a process that began in 2012. During that period there were still occasional issues to deal with concerning Lockerbie – an investigation that seems doomed to go on and on. The other outstanding case at the time was the attempt by al-Qaeda to blow up airliners using explosive concealed in printer cartridges. But by then my days as a front-line casework officer were long gone and a new generation of FEL scientists had taken up the baton that I was handing on.

Afterword

I retired from the Forensic Explosives Laboratory two days after my sixtieth birthday, and drove out of the Fort for the last time on 15 May 2013, after working there for twenty-six years.

It was a strange feeling. Uppermost in my mind was the thought that I was now free from the responsibility of work, and I could concentrate on giving back to Vanessa all the things that she had missed due to the demands of my job. And we had many plans about how we wanted to spend this new part of our lives together.

This was really all I wanted to do. I had been looking forward to it for at least the last two or three years of my time at the FEL and I had absolutely no sense of loss at not having to go back there the next day. And yet . . . I still had to pull over. Halfway down the road to the Fort entrance, I sat for a minute or two, letting it sink in: I would not be coming this way again.

I thought back over my time at the FEL, from my earliest cases, many of them involving the work of the IRA, and

then, more recently, the altogether more sinister and dangerous threat of Islamic extremist terrorists. I had loved being
a casework officer, being set to work on a new mystery,
trying to piece together what a bomber had done and helping the police understand who they might be looking for.
Or trying to come to grips with a completely new explosive
combination, some of which were remarkably ingenious.

But it struck me then that it wasn't really the thrill of
the investigative process that was exerting a pull on me –
it was the people I had worked with. It was a wonderful
group that has continued to develop and improve the contribution of the FEL, providing a service the need for which
is not going to diminish any time soon.

We had all lived through a challenging period, when the
FEL was pushed as never before, and this team played a
crucial role in the UK's response to multiple threats, helping to convict perpetrators and stop others from carrying
out similar acts of violence. We never worked in isolation,
though, and just as important were our colleagues in the
police, the army's EOD operators, and experts in other
forensic disciplines.

I put the car in gear and headed home to start the next
chapter of our lives – which was already a little bittersweet.
After her diagnosis back in 2004, Vanessa had finally been
declared free of breast cancer in 2011 after a particularly
tough few years of treatment. A year later, after a trip to
see friends in Oregon, she had felt unwell when we stopped

overnight at a spectacular place called Timberline Lodge, high up on a volcano in the Rockies. We didn't think too much about it, but when we got back home she went to the doctor for a check-up – and we were devastated to find out that the cancer had returned, some in the lungs and some in her bones. We were told it could be controlled and slowed down but it could not be cured. Nevertheless the doctors were hopeful that Vanessa would enjoy a further five years of good quality of life.

This gave me every incentive to push forward my exit from the FEL and I was still hopeful we would have plenty of time together in retirement. But just six months after I drove out of the Fort for the last time, and just after we had returned from a ten-day trip on the Danube, she suddenly went downhill and was admitted to hospital by ambulance. I followed in my own car with some overnight things for her, but by the time I got there Vanessa was unconscious, and thirty-six hours later she died.

This hit me hard. I had lost the love of my life and all my retirement plans – which included enjoying a motor-boat we had bought together – had vanished like so much smoke. For a while I was at a loss to know how to go on. But I had always liked writing, and, over time, as a form of therapy as much as anything else, I started jotting down little bits and pieces, nothing to do with work, just personal stuff, but it seemed to help a bit. Then I started to wonder if I could write something a bit more focused about what I had been doing during all those years at the FEL. It occurred to me that I had never really looked back or considered my career in any sort of reflective way, or ever even really talked about it much with friends or family.

And that is how I came to write this book. It was never planned, it just sort of happened. But now that I've done it I'm quite pleased, because it has opened my eyes to some things I was not previously aware of, some good and some not so good, but all beneficial in some way. I was enormously helped by the fact that I kept detailed notes of all my cases, and it was great fun for me to try to re-create the different challenges that each of them presented.

These days everyone is on a personal journey of some kind. Actually, mine is about someone who loved what he did, and my career experiences never led me into some dark corner of crisis, but perhaps a bit of personal reflection and insight at the time would have been a good thing. Writing this book has helped me realise that my experiences, not least on 7/7, did have an effect on me and left a mark that I was not aware of at the time.

Sadly, I suspect that Vanessa saw something of what I didn't – another cross she had to bear, and some guilt to carry for me, but at least I know it now. I don't think anyone could enter that tunnel and witness what we did that day and not feel – for years afterwards – the intrusive memories pushing in on their subconscious. One or two images apart, I have managed to process it all and put it

Afterword

largely behind me, but I will never forget the people who died down there on a day when their commute to work was so brutally interrupted.

Up until now the role of the forensic explosives scientist has gone largely unheralded. I hope this account – which covers less than one-fifth of all the cases I worked on – will help to increase public awareness of the vital work that is done in this area by those anonymous-looking men and women in white suits who we all see in news coverage at the scenes of terrorist attacks and other disasters where explosives may be involved.

Acknowledgements

Just as forensic science is a team effort, both within its own field and among other agencies, so too is writing a book – or it was for this book anyway. First and foremost, my thanks go to Ed Gorman, a journalist and former Deputy Head of News at *The Times* newspaper. It is his skill as a writer in transforming my dry and unfocused ramblings into a coherent set of fascinating stories that has made this book into something people would actually want to read. More than that, for me personally, he turned what might have become a bit of a chore into a hugely enjoyable challenge and collaborative effort that I already miss now that it's over.

Of course, I didn't come across Ed by accident – that was down to Mark Lucas at The Soho Agency, who has guided my every step into the world of publishing with unfailing good humour and wisdom, encouraging and believing in this project from the start. And then finding, persuading and likewise enthusing my publisher, Iain MacGregor at Headline, to take a risk with me and turn the project into a real book.

EXPLOSIVE

But where did the first tiny seed for this spring from? That came from a sharp-eyed TV producer at True Stories Productions, Julie Davies, who happened to read a rough-and-ready self-published book I had previously written, called *7/7 and 21/7 – Delving into Room 101*. She saw some potential there and encouraged me to consider writing a more comprehensive account of my career as a forensic scientist, eventually culminating in my introduction to Mark Lucas – and so the project was born. Without any one of those people, this book would not have happened, and I am immensely grateful to them all for their help and encouragement.

Then, of course, there are the indirect helpers; three in particular being my sister, Sue, and friends Alan and Steve, for their thoughts and advice on reading a few early chapters, each useful and different in their own ways. Steve deserves a special mention for his direct, not to say blunt, approach to literary criticism, at one point suggesting the style was a little 'posh'. Not quite how he put it, but valid and attended to nevertheless, and I was happy to accept it as a term of endearment.

Just as important are the many people from my own explosives forensic world, who were an intrinsic part of many of the stories in this book, to a man and woman, all crucial to the work that was done and is being done today. They were and are a wonderful team and it is my privilege to have worked with them. I reserve a special mention for

Acknowledgements

Tom Hayes, who, more than anyone, was a mentor to me, and sadly left the FEL long before I (or most other people) expected him to. Of all the people I have known in the forensics world, he was the one I most aspired to compare myself to.

Finally there is my late wife, Vanessa and my son, Andrew. Without Vanessa's love, understanding and unstinting support through some difficult times, I would be a lesser person than I am today, and my life and career would have been very different. And my son, who figures briefly in the book as a young child, has always supported me, for which I am hugely grateful, even though my job may at times have seemed to take priority over his needs. To him I say – Nog still has pride of place on my bedside table to this day.

Chesterfield, Derbyshire
December 2020

Glossary

AAIB – Air Accident Investigation Branch. British aircraft crash investigation agency.

Al-Qaeda – A network of Islamic extremists founded by Osama bin Laden in 1988

BLEVE – Boiling-liquid expanding-vapour explosion. A form of fuel-air explosion.

DNA – Deoxyribonucleic acid. A part of all known life forms' genetic material.

DNT – Dinitrotoluene. A high explosive, common as a by-product in TNT, also sometimes used in its own right in types of ammunition.

Dstl – Defence Science and Technology Laboratory, part of the Ministry of Defence.

EOD – Explosive ordnance disposal. Bomb disposal.

Explosive testing kits – FEL-produced kits to collect explosives traces or residues for later analysis in the laboratory.

EXPO – a Metropolitan Police bomb disposal officer.

Glossary

FBI – Federal Bureau of Investigation. American law enforcement agency.

FEL – Forensic Explosives Laboratory.

Gasometer – A large, old-style, gas holder with sections that moved up and down depending on how full it was. No longer used in this country.

HMTD – Hexamethylene triperoxide diamene. A very sensitive explosive that is easily detonated by heat, shock or friction.

HSE – Health and Safety Executive.

IRA – Irish Republican Army

IRMS – Isotope-ratio mass spectrometry. A method of chemical analysis.

Memo-park timer – a brand of small clockwork timer that used to be commonly used by people parked at a parking meter, to set an alarm to remind them that the meter was about to run out. You set it simply by twisting its dial to the required time, from where it would unwind until it ran out and rang a buzzer.

MI5 – The domestic security service, a British intelligence agency.

MoD – Ministry of Defence.

PE4 – Standard British military plastic demolition explosive.

PETN – Pentaerthyritol tetranitrate. Commercially-made explosive used in many kinds of explosive formulations, including detonators and detonating cords.

EXPLOSIVE

RDX – Commercially-made explosive used in many kinds of plastic and military explosive products. Also called Royal Demolition eXplosive, cyclonite, cyclotrimethylene trinitramine, amongst many other names.

SCCRC – Scottish Criminal Cases Review Commission.

SO13 – The anti-terrorist branch of the Metropolitan Police.

SO15 – The anti-terrorist branch of the Metropolitan Police, renamed in 2006, after it was merged with SO12, otherwise known as the Special Branch.

Swab (swabbing) – a process of rubbing a solvent-moistened cotton wool ball over a hard surface to extract small particles of explosive for later analysis in the laboratory.

TATP – Triacetone triperoxide. A very sensitive explosive that is easily detonated by heat, shock or friction.

TNT – Trinitrotoluene. A common military high explosive used in many kinds of ordnance, e.g. grenades, artillery shells and bombs.

TPU – Time and Power Unit, a device to remotely detonate an explosive, usually after a preset delay.

Index

Index

Index

Index

Index

EXPLOSIVE

Index

Toshiba 31
Toshiba radio cassette RT-8016 30–2,
   34, 35
Tovey, David 187–8
trace lab, cleanliness protocols 169–70
training 43
Treacy, Colman, QC 199
triacetone-triperoxide 151–7
United States of America 70
Unnatural Causes (Shepherd) 214
unpredictable substances 274
Utah, University of 236–7

vapour cloud explosion 248
Vaughn, Keith 83, 86–7, 93
victims 43
   interviews 49–51
Victoria Station bomb 106–7

Warrington gas works bombing 78,
   128–43
   aims 135
   arrests 129
   blast site 131–3
   bomb 131–2
   bombs placed 129, 132–3
   convictions 137–43
   explosion 129–30
   gas clouds 133–7, 138–41
   gas holders 128
   incendiary devices 131, 132, 134
   investigation 130–7
   IRA retaliations 130–1
   litterbin bombs 130–1
   trial 137–43
Watson, Steven 160, 161–2
Welch, Thomas J. 96
White City 205
Wilkes, Jonathan 179–88
   bomb construction 183–5, 188
   bombing campaign 180–2

linked to bombs 185–6
   motivation 186, 187
   sentence 186–7
   target 187
   and Tovey 187–8
   trial 186
Wiltshire car bomb 41–60
   army bomb disposal 45
   bomb confirmed 51–2
   and Bristol car bomb 53–5
   car removed 51
   cost 49
   CT assigned case 41–2
Wiltshire car bomb (*cont.*)
   damage 46–7, 48
   debris 49
   detonator 56
   device 56–9
   evidence points to bomb 48–9
   explosive 55–6
   fingerprint evidence 59
   first impressions 44–6
   ground underneath 51–2
   initial assessment 46–8
   journey to 43–4
   petrol fire 60
   positioning 57
   smell 44
   tearing pattern 48
   victim interview 49–51
Winterslow 44
witness plates 181
witnesses, reliable 43
Woolwich Crown Court 247–8, 283,
   298
World Zionist Organisation 148

X-ray imaging 240

Yorkshire 146
Yusuf (forensic explosive scientist) 220

Picture Credits